A WAY FROM DARKNESS

FOREWORD

A WAY FROM DARKNESS

My story of addiction, recovery, and yoga

TAYLOR HUNT

A Way from Darkness

My story of addiction, recovery, and yoga

First published in 2016 by Ekam Publishing

Copyright © 2016 Taylor Hunt

All rights reserved.

ISBN-13: 978-0692638392

ISBN-10: 0692638393

Cover artwork: Amber Fogel

Design: Natalie Kleoudis

Printed in The United States of America

awayfromdarkness.com

I dedicate this book to the Ashtanga yoga lineage and to all of those suffering from alcoholism and drug addiction.

ACKNOWLEDGMENTS

Jessica, thank you for giving me endless love and support in all of my endeavors. Makayla and Isaiah, thank you for making me a dad and for showing me how to love unconditionally. Know that it is only because of the events described in this book that I am able to share my life with you today.

R. Sharath Jois, thank you for being a great example for me to aspire to. Your presence in my life means more to me than you will ever know.

Matthew Darling, thank you for being my big brother in sobriety and a guiding light on my Ashtanga path.

Laruga Glaser, thank you for inspiring me to go deeper into my practice. I will always cherish the time that I spent practicing with you.

Joanie Delph, thank you for being my yoga mom and for opening the door to a whole new way of living.

Sree Aswath, thank you for helping me deepen my yoga studies and being a part of my story.

Dawn Blevins, Amber Fogel, Nicole DeFazio, Natalie Kleoudis, Brett McLaughlin, Marsha Mueller, Melanie Stein, Paula McCaw, Margot Connor, Jo Dee Davis, and Erin Eichel, thank you for your contributions to the process. Without your input, there is no way this book would exist. Thank you for your support.

CONTENTS

It was Christmas morning, 2013, when I walked up the steps from my second-floor apartment to the apartment where Taylor always stays with his family in Mysore. It was my first trip to India, and I woke up lonely and missing my husband. Jess and Taylor welcomed me inside, and we sat on the floor talking while eating cheese and crackers. Their apartment had a warmth that made it an inviting gathering place.

Taylor had been my teacher for six months before he and his family left for their three-month stay in India. I joined them for the third month. Jess and Taylor had spent the past several weeks showing me around and helping me adjust to life in India and, on that day, they made me feel like family. It was a testament to their caring natures and to Taylor's fervent commitment to each of his students.

In August of the following year, Taylor and I met for coffee and he asked me to help him write his memoir. At that point, he had been publically sharing his past struggles with alcoholism and drug addiction for only a couple of months. I didn't know much about his story beyond that he was in recovery and that yoga was a major part of his journey toward healing. After he warned me that the rest of the story contained a great deal of darkness, we both spent some time separately contemplating the potential impact on our teacher-student relationship. In the Ashtanga yoga tradition, we practice with our teachers six days a week, often before sunrise. They witness all of our highs and lows, from the joy of doing a difficult posture for the first time to the days when we can do little more than lie in a tearful sweaty heap on the shala floor. From that, they frequently intuit what is going on in our lives off the mats without any words being spoken. It's a deep bond that requires mutual trust and respect. Taylor and I already had that, but we knew that writing his memoir together would bring a new level of intensity and significance to our relationship.

As we began the project, I couldn't help but remember when, on that same trip to Mysore, I accidently sat down in a twelve-step recovery meeting that Jess and Taylor were attending on the patio. Everyone was incredibly kind when they let me know what was going on. I don't think anyone gave a second thought to my mistake, but I felt terrible about rudely barging into a gathering where I didn't belong. What I didn't realize at the time was that life was awkwardly foreshadowing what was to come. Working on this book sometimes felt similar to that incident, except that Taylor invited me to sit down and listen. In order to fully understand his experiences, I often had to ask questions that I thought sounded impolite and intrusive. I wondered if I had again barged into a place where I didn't belong.

It turned out, though, that I did belong because I had much to learn from Taylor's story, which I think is true for everyone who reads it. Our year of working on the book coincided with my year of contemplating whether I was meant to be a yoga teacher. When Taylor asked me to assist him in the shala, I quickly learned that helping other students felt very natural to me. But I wasn't convinced I was supposed to be a teacher in my own right. I spent the entire year fighting against the path that was clearly opening before me because it didn't fit neatly into my own plans and because I didn't believe I was ready. A recurring message in Taylor's story is the importance of surrender and overcoming self-doubt. As the book took shape, I couldn't escape the obvious—Taylor's message related directly to my own life. I just needed to apply it. Taylor likes to say that there are no coincidences in life. I think the way our two paths converged confirms that.

For those of us who have not been personally touched by addiction, it can seem like a distant problem that is difficult to comprehend. Before hearing Taylor's story, I knew that addiction was a disease and not a moral failing, but I had no concept of its power and its persistence. Taylor offers us a window into the life of an addict and invites us to find compassion for all who are suffering from the disease. To those who are currently battling addiction, or struggling in some other way, Taylor offers a message of hope that healing and transformation are possible and that a better life awaits. As we wrote this book, Taylor opened his heart and soul to me, without reserve. On the pages that follow, he opens them to you as well.

DAWN BLEVINS, PH.D.
KPJAYI Level II Authorized Ashtanga Teacher

AUTHOR'S NOTE

The first part of this memoir recounts a time when I was abusing drugs and alcohol. The events that are portrayed are recollected to the best of my ability. Some names have been changed to protect anonymity.

I'm holding my own private wake to honor the life we've had as a family. It's over now and I don't know what the future holds. We're all starting anew. I'm dressed nicely for this event, but I feel dirty all over. I need to wash the filth and the pain away. I find a fifth of Beefeater in the basement and take a drink for the first time in my life. I'm shocked by the harshness of the gin and have to brace myself before I can swallow more. It's so gross, like drinking an evergreen tree, but I'm not interested in stopping. Fuck it. I'm doing whatever it takes to get away from these feelings. I would drink anything, do any drug, just to escape and hide at this point. I don't care if it tastes like shit or destroys me. I don't want to feel any of this.

There are twenty people at my house. A few are good friends who understand what I'm going through, but the others are just acquaintances. I overhear someone's telephone conversation but can't hold onto any of the words. I can feel the blackout coming on. I look out the window and see the leaves falling as a few friends smoke weed in the backyard. I'm holding tightly to the bottle as I continue to chug. I remember we're supposed to be leaving for a football game soon.

"You need to slow down. What's wrong with you?"

I keep drinking until I begin to slur my words. My hair is coming undone. My Abercrombie flannel is now only partially tucked into my carpenter jeans. My lips are becoming loose and I'm spewing sadness all over. I'm so distraught that I don't even know what I'm saying. They are words that should be shared with a counselor, not my drunk friends. People are still drinking and having a good time, but I'm becoming too much to handle.

"Taylor's being all emotional. He's gone over the edge."

"This is just too sloppy."

"I'm out of here. I don't need this drama."

Disembodied voices swirl above me as I lie comatose on the beige carpet in our living room. The photos of our former family mock me from the shelves above the fireplace. I watch as more friends walk out the door. I'm not sure who's still there to hand me a metal pot, but I welcome the coolness as I put my head into it. Everything goes dark.

"Taylor! Taylor! What's going on?" I'm jolted out of the quiet blackness of my pot as I hear my mom's panicked sobbing above me. She's been drinking too, holding her own wake, and has just arrived home to find me crumpled on the floor. We both ran from the sadness that was too much to bear tonight. Neither of us agreed to the dissolution of our family. I notice I'm covered in sweat and I feel immediate *regret. I never want to hear her say my name in that voice again. She's convinced I'm dying and calls her friend Bev for help. I feel my mom lift my head and cradle it in her hands as Bev's boyfriend Tony stands over me, arms crossed.*

"I think he's just drunk. You don't need to worry about him."

My mom is relieved but still crying when she leaves me alone on the floor. I have a splitting headache. I'm getting nauseous and the dry heaves begin. The pot is empty, but I'm drowning in guilt, shame, and remorse.

CHAPTER 1

COMING UNDONE

On the day my parents' divorce was finalized, my whole life changed. I didn't go to court with them or witness any of the proceedings, but I knew what was happening. I felt empty, scared, and alone all day. Anxiety and pressure swelled inside of me until I cried tears of confusion and of the unknown. I was fifteen and I no longer had any idea what my life was going to look like from day to day. *Everything is changing.*

When Mom got home from court, she didn't know how to deal with her feelings either. I heard her sniffle from crying as she got dressed up. She went out with her friends and left me home by myself. Instead of sitting down to talk and comfort each other, we both chose to go our separate ways, like two ships passing in the night. I had never felt so alone and confused.

I threw a party because I felt like getting into trouble instead of facing what was going on inside. I wanted to be numb and to escape. I didn't know how to deal with the pain, so I guessed that drinking would take it away. I drank the bottle of Beefeater because it was the only bottle of liquor in the house. I found it covered in cobwebs on top of the basement fridge. It was left over from one of my parents' past gatherings. As soon as I tasted it, I knew why it was still there. *This stuff tastes like shit.* I forced myself to swallow each gulp through sheer willpower because I wanted to run away from reality. I wanted to know what being drunk was like because I was certain it was better than being myself, even though I didn't know who that was.

From a young age, I had low self-esteem and never believed that people really liked me. That made me anxious and unable to connect with anyone. I didn't have any good friends who I felt comfortable talking to about my problems, especially the divorce. The alcohol suddenly made me stop caring what anyone else thought. My inhibitions were gone and I felt like it was acceptable to express my feelings. Among my group of friends, that wouldn't have been comfortable for me in any other context. Drinking took away my anxiety and made the weight of my parents' divorce feel lighter. I breathed a deep sigh of relief.

During the party, I boasted to my friends about my newfound freedom since Dad wasn't around anymore. I was laughing, but inside, I was so sad. My friends weren't drinking as hard as I was and they didn't know what was going on as they watched me unravel. On the outside, I seemed to have everything together. But as soon as I started drinking, my emotions surrounding the divorce and my family began to surface. Eventually I got drunk enough that I couldn't pretend anymore. The floodgates opened and tears streamed down my face.

"Pour me another shot."

"Another shot."

"Taylor, put the bottle down. You don't need to go that fast."

"Another."

I don't remember anything until I woke up on the living room floor with my head in that pot. *How did I get here? Why did I do that?* I immediately felt guilty that I let down my guard and divulged the secret that my family had been destroyed and my whole world was crashing down around me. I was ashamed because I was not comfortable with being so emotional around other people. I thought I was supposed to be tougher than that. I already felt bad about myself, and my very public response to the divorce made it even worse. I experienced remorse because I wished none of it had happened. I needed to grieve over the fact that my family as I knew it no longer existed. But instead of taking a step toward healthy behavior and healing, I took my first step towards alcoholism and darkness. I felt loneliness. I got drunk. I spewed my emotions onto whoever was around. I felt incredible guilt, shame, and remorse for drinking too much. That was my new normal.

My parents divorced because Dad was having an affair. It began when I was twelve and it shifted our family dynamics. Around the same time, Dad started a produce business and began working eighty or more hours per week. He used his long work hours to hide the affair from us. He and Mom steadily grew further and further apart. Dad distanced himself from me and my two sisters as well. His once constant presence in our lives became sporadic. I didn't understand why, at first.

I was in my room one Friday night, after Mom went to bed, when I heard the phone ring. I ran to another room and picked up at the same time Dad picked up downstairs. I heard a woman's voice. Dad must have heard me breathing. He immediately told me to hang up because it was Mark, one of his employees. But I had no doubt that I heard a female voice. I walked back to my room wondering why Dad would lie to me. I couldn't shake the feeling of suspicion that crept over me.

A few weekends later, my older sister Amber was out partying with her friends when she walked into a restaurant and saw Dad dining with a blonde woman. Amber called home and was sobbing when I answered the phone.

"Put Mom on the phone."

"She's in bed. What do you need?"

"Give Mom the phone now!"

"Why?"

"I just saw Dad cheating on Mom! He's at dinner with another woman!"

Amber was hysterical and I was in shock as I passed the phone. Mom had been suspicious for a while. A neighbor left a letter in our mailbox one day saying the same thing Amber just said. Dad had been spotted out with another woman. Dad wouldn't own up to it though. Instead, he prolonged the relationship with Mom and made everything worse. As soon as Mom heard Amber on the line, all of her suspicions were confirmed.

Amber discovered Dad's affair about a year before I took my first drink. I resisted believing the truth about Dad for as long as possible. The facts were playing out right in front of my eyes, but it was a puzzle inside my head. Dad was the only person I really felt connected to at the time, but I was confused about what he was up to. I didn't understand his plan. He tried to spare me pain by not having the tough conversation he needed to have with me. I was so confused.

At fifteen, I couldn't understand the impact the divorce would have on me. The timing was significant because it happened at the age when I was becoming a man. Dad simply wasn't available for me anymore. The presence I was used to disappeared. After he moved out, I only saw him for a few hours each weekend. We always met at a restaurant or the mall, activities that never lasted the entire day. He didn't want to take my sisters and me to his new home, so those short visits were the only time we had together during my last three years of high school. That was a sharp contrast to the golf games and daily family meals we used to share. If I called him during the week, it felt like I was talking to a stranger. I didn't know him anymore. In my heart, our connection was lost.

I felt like my life had become a fictional story because Dad wasn't who I had believed him to be. Everything about the affair felt dirty and gross. Dad violated the trust in our family and I resented him for it. Dad told us he was moving out as we sat at dinner one night. He explained that he was going to live at another woman's house and that she had three kids of her own. I felt like I was being replaced. Dad shifted from my closest friend to someone whose trustworthiness I questioned. He left us with the wreckage of his past life while he moved on and started a whole new life with a new family. My best friend became the person who caused me the most pain.

Mom and Dad fought a constant battle for a few years before the divorce. I was the primary witness to it because my little sister Amanda was still too young to understand what was going on, and Amber was away serving in the U.S. Marine Corps. Watching their marriage fall apart shattered me. Dad's absence caused Mom's mental state to deteriorate and she was plunged into a sea of anxiety and depression. Dad had been the head of our family. He gave direction and carved out a life for us. The vision came from him. Mom was the support person who sustained the life he created. In Dad's absence, it was not clear what our family should look like. We were like a ship without a rudder. Mom didn't know how to be the leader. She was a mess. I witnessed her rip apart her once beautifully manicured fingernails out of anxiety. The life she knew was over, and the mom I knew was gone.

In happier times, Mom was the stereotypical stay-at-home suburban mom. Raising us and managing the household was her life's work and she enjoyed it. She was meticulous with the finances. Her couponing and penny-pinching contrasted with Dad's free-spending ways. Mom kept the checkbook balanced while Dad paid cash for everything. He always carried a huge rubberbanded wad of cash in his pocket and kept one in the car too. It drove Mom nuts.

Mom was nurturing and closely involved in the lives of her children. She tutored us and made sure our homework was always done, met with our teachers, and drove us wherever we needed to go. Mom coddled us more than Dad did, but she was also good at nagging us until we did all of the things we didn't want to do. She was the taskmaster and was always engaged and present with us.

Family was the most important thing to Mom and it gave her purpose. We were her entire life.

Before the affair, Mom was open and always available to talk. Afterward, she was still completely committed to us, but she was no longer fully present. Her mind was somewhere else. The burden of the affair weighed her down. Her pride was crushed and she was ashamed about losing her twenty-five-year marriage. She worried about what people would think of her. I could see in Mom's face that the circumstances were killing her. She was consumed by fear about the future and worry over what it would hold for all of us without Dad. Her sadness and withdrawal closed her off and the open communication we once enjoyed ended. The entire situation was a shitshow and I just needed someone to talk to about all of it. But I had no one.

Dad was a cool person to hang around with, but he wasn't available to have the tough conversations I needed to have with him. He was good at supporting his children monetarily, but not psychologically or emotionally. Dad never asked how I was feeling or helped ease the transition into my new post-divorce life. Talking about those things wasn't "macho" in his mind. Because Dad, my only role model, wasn't in touch with his feelings, I didn't know how to face my own emotions.

I thought Dad would be angry about my first drunken night and we would have to talk about things. The morning after, Mom called Dad to come over because he was always the one who punished us. He wasn't allowed in the house anymore, so when he arrived, Mom told me to go outside. I found Dad standing in the garage. The first thing he said to me was, "Hey, I heard you had a little too much fun last night."

"Yeah." I tried to tell him that I was confused and trying to figure out what was going on with our family, but he shut me down.

"Don't do that again because it will worry your mom."

"Alright."

Then he gave me a fistbump as he said, "Take care of yourself and don't let that happen again." It was the day after the divorce and Dad didn't even give me a hug. He was distant and refused to engage with me. I was withdrawn too because I felt different around Dad than I had before. Something in me had changed. Part of my innocence was gone, and with that loss, I took my first step toward addiction.

I actually wanted consequences for my drinking because it would mean he would have to have a longer conversation with me. I wanted the attention. We didn't even have a sit down talk. When I saw him standing in the garage, I knew he wouldn't be staying for long. Dad tried to be my friend instead of lecturing me about drinking. He didn't acknowledge that my behavior was about the divorce. I wanted to talk about what was going on and tell him why I was angry. As usual, Dad didn't want to talk about feelings. He was gone in ten minutes and I was left standing by myself. *What the hell is going on?*

I tried talking to Dad about the divorce other times, still with no luck. When I brought it up, he said, "You have to get over this. I'm over it. We have to move forward." Dad was concerned about my well-being and thought that was the best advice he could give me. But I couldn't get over the divorce because I was crushed. Mom wasn't over it either, but she was too sad to talk about it.

I knew the day of the divorce was coming, but there was nothing that could have prepared me for the end of my parents' marriage. Dad's energy was no longer present in the house, and that left a huge void. He had filled an integral and charismatic role in the family. Even though he'd been working a lot to build his business, he was still engaged with us and cared about our lives. After the divorce, there was an emptiness that made me think I needed to fill his shoes. Dad didn't expect me to step up and do that, but I felt pressure to do it anyway.

Mom was in crisis and could no longer take care of herself. I watched her struggle as she suddenly had to go back to work after twenty years. She was only making eight dollars an hour working at a gym. I needed money, but I couldn't ask Mom for it because she didn't have much. I didn't want to be a burden on her. Dad would give me a hundred bucks when I saw him, but he usually wasn't around to ask when I needed something. I got a job as a cook because it was the highest paying job I could find. I made fourteen dollars an hour and worked forty hours a week so I could buy the things I needed and help Mom out with the household bills. I felt an enormous responsibility to help Mom take care of Amanda and keep things going at home. It was too much of a burden for me to bear at age fifteen, but I felt like I had no other choice.

I told Mom that she needed to go back to school or do something to make more money because I couldn't be the man of the house. Nothing changed though. I continued working a lot so I could have money in the bank. It felt natural to work so hard. It distracted me from the pain I wanted to avoid. It gave me a purpose. I needed to help Mom keep everything together, even at the cost of my own well-being and healing. I was no longer a kid.

My family meant everything to me. We spent lots of time together and they provided the balance that was in my life. Losing that made me angry. I was angry about my parents' fighting, I was angry about Dad's deception, and I was angry about Mom's response to the situation. I acted aggressively toward both of them because the divorce was their fault. I cried out for help by drinking because I thought it would get me into trouble. I wanted them to know that and I wanted their attention, but they didn't get the message. I believed my once attentive parents had abandoned me. I felt utterly alone.

I attempted to fill that void with other people. I tried to forget about Dad's absence by surrounding myself with as many friends as possible. That wasn't hard for me because I was a chameleon who could fit in with everyone. I continued to throw parties at my house. My behavior at those parties was reckless and dangerous because I was seeking attention, even if it was negative.

The parties did get me accepted into the popular crowd. I went to a suburban high school where most of the kids wore designer clothes and drove nice cars. The girls all had fake tans and highlighted hair. Our parents were doctors, lawyers, and business owners. It was a new money crowd and it was cliquey and gossipy. Thanks to my low self-esteem, the environment was toxic. There was so much judgment from everyone. Image was everything and everyone was jockeying to be number one, including me. I was trying to be someone. I sought power through popularity. I wanted to be wanted by others since I didn't feel nurtured at home anymore.

Playing the popularity game required me to wear a mask because I had always been more of a loner. As a small child, I didn't really want to play with anyone. I used to hide out in my closet a lot. When Amber or my parents looked for me, they could find me shut inside, playing by myself in the dark. I was happy there. Being alone didn't feel lonely. Once my family life crumbled, I started seeking connection with others, but I'd never developed the personal skills to build close relationships. Social interactions were awkward and I never really felt like I was a part of things when I was with my friends. It seemed like everyone else had something I wanted. I thought they had a playbook to life that told them how to be and what to do. I was continually searching for that kind of direction.

Not knowing what else to do, I spent the rest of my high school years partying. My friends and I took over the house while Mom spent her time at the bar. I don't even know where Amanda was during that time, or who was taking care of her. I took advantage of Mom's absence and invited people over all the time. On any given day, there might have been as many as thirty cars parked on our street. The neighbors saw what was going on at our house, but no one stopped me.

When I wasn't partying, home life continued to suck. My world was torn apart, but I was trying desperately to keep it together so that Mom, Amanda, and I would be alright. *How can I help Mom? How do I get her to care about us again? How do I get Dad to care about us again? Is it even possible?* Dad had always taught me that I couldn't have anything that wasn't earned. While my friends' fathers might try to talk the basketball coach into giving their sons more playing time, Dad had a different perspective.

"If you want something, you have to get it for yourself. I'll support you, but you have to do the work. You have to earn it."

I was pissed off about the divorce, so I went to work and tried to earn my place in the world like Dad had drilled into my head. *Work your ass off. Your family needs you. Quit whining and just do it.* I was trying to save what was left of my family, but I didn't feel like I was enough to fill Dad's shoes. It was too much and I was miserable. The only break I had from it was when I drank.

I couldn't help longing for the time before Dad's affair. Things were never perfect in our family, but it was functional. Amber, Amanda, and I all walked to the beat of our own drummers because of our age differences. We were each seven years apart, so we each felt a little bit like an only child. That didn't change after the divorce. What I really missed was time with my parents. Mom used to cook dinner every night and after Dad arrived home from work, we all ate together around our oval dining room table. Family time was always important. Even though Dad was busy with work, when he was home with us, he was really present. He went out of his way to be at my baseball and basketball games as well as all of the other important events Dads are supposed to attend. He and I spent lots of time tossing a baseball and playing golf together. We were two buddies who had a lot of fun.

In the summer months, I spent all of my time practicing at the golf course. I was serious about improving my game and Dad was committed to helping me do that. He used to meet me there to play a round every evening after he got off work. There was a whole group of father-son pairs who played together. Sometimes we had putting contests while our dads bet on who was going to win. It was highly competitive, which suited Dad's personality. He was the most competitive person I knew. We used to coach each other through the round each evening. Dad had much more experience than me, but he always appreciated having an extra set of eyes on his game. We spent so much time on that golf course, and it bonded us.

Those days were suddenly gone and Dad was living with his new family. Eventually, I had to meet Donna, the person who broke up my home and became my stepmom. She was a blonde Italian woman who wanted to hug and kiss me every time I saw her. I didn't understand her behavior and it made me uncomfortable. I would have preferred to strangle her. I pinned all of the blame for my parents' divorce on Donna instead of Dad because I still wanted to have a relationship with him. I didn't want to be angry with Dad, so I directed all of the anger that was boiling up inside of me toward her. I was furious and I had no one to talk to about it.

As a kid from the suburbs, I was shocked when I saw Donna's house for the first time. It was an old house on the west side of town that smelled like stale well water, and it still had laundry lines hanging outside. Dad's car was worth more than her house. The day I first saw Donna's house I decided she was a gold digger. *This is an old fucking house. How could Dad leave us and our nice house for this shithole?* But I was so furious with her that I would have hated her house, no matter how nice it was. Donna's presence in Dad's life was a slap in the face that stung even more once I met her three kids. I hated all of them. I still couldn't deal with my parents' divorce, so I definitely didn't want to interact with the new people in Dad's life. I didn't want to be a part of their family and I didn't want them to be a part of my family. I only wanted my family back. I worried there was no longer a place for me in Dad's heart.

I increased the amount of alcohol I drank to fill the emptiness. I needed to know who I was supposed to be, but without Dad around to show me the way, I was lost. Many of the adults in my life told me I had a lot of potential and could be good at anything I set my mind to. I disagreed and could feel the pressure of those high expectations. *How could I ever measure up to that?* I didn't feel like the external qualities people saw in me matched the way I felt about myself inside. I didn't feel like I was good enough, and I looked for validation in the approval of others. I was unsure of myself. *I don't even know who I am, but I'm trying to find my way.* I thought I might have been responsible for Dad leaving and that made me highly emotional, although I had no outlet for my feelings. As a result, the negative aspects of my character were magnified. I didn't like me. I said horrible things to myself. I never would have allowed anyone else to speak to me that way. My character reflected my negative self-image. I was self-centered, impulsive, and arrogant. I was emotionally stunted and socially awkward.

I felt like a wreck who was on a constant emotional roller coaster ride. But people didn't know that about me because I wore a very convincing mask. Hearing I had potential was a burden for me. It made me feel like I had to be perfect. When I drank, I let go of the need to be perfect. It was a huge relief.

I wake up groggy and hung over. It's 10:00 on Friday morning. I'm skipping school for the weekly beer run. We have a system. On Thursday, we take everyone's order and collect the money. A few of us drive to the west side around 11:00 on Friday. It's an hour round trip, but we know Malik at the drive-through will sell beer to us. He doesn't care that we have shitty fake IDs. Mine is just a slip of paper with a different birthday wedged in between the clear plastic of my wallet and my real driver's license. Malik knows what we're doing. He's not stupid.

Scott, Michael, Brian, and I make the trip today. We buy three hundred dollars' worth of beer. We fill Michael's trunk and the back of Scott's truck with it. By 2:00, we are already wasted on Michael's front porch. I happen to notice a green Infiniti drive slowly by. As we smoke cigarettes and weed, we decide to move the party to Scott's house before Michael's mom gets home.

I'm riding in Michael's copper Mitsubishi Eclipse. We call it The Penny. It sticks out like a sore thumb wherever Michael goes. I glance in the side mirror and swear I see the same green Infiniti behind us. "Dude, you're just being paranoid," Michael tells me.

We pull up at Scott's house and begin unloading the twenty-four packs of beer to take inside. Just as I'm about to open a can, I see the green Infiniti barreling toward us. What the hell is going on? I assume we're about to be robbed. I throw the beer that's in my hand back into the trunk when a guy steps out of the car and yells, "Freeze! Dublin Police!"

I slam the trunk shut and take off running. I'm sprinting as fast as my long legs can possibly take me. Later, Brian tells me I looked like a deer. I just keep running. I only stop a couple of times to hide in bushes when I think someone is following me. Still drunk, I arrive at my girlfriend's house, six miles away.

I'm out of breath when I explain the situation. "The cops are after me. They busted us for drinking." She lets me inside and tells me I can sleep in the basement. I collapse on her couch in a drunk heap of exhaustion.

CHAPTER 2

DOUBLE LIFE

Despite my drinking, I always went to school and I managed to do really well. I never had to study for anything, even though I often went to school drunk or hung over. I drank with my friends before school and after school, but I was good at keeping up appearances. I even found myself in some leadership roles. I was on the student council and I was the executive producer for the school TV show. Although I was a weekend warrior in the party scene and was in the process of becoming a raging alcoholic, I was still able to impress my teachers for a while. But that became more difficult as partying filled more and more of my time. I struggled to maintain my double life.

I began to make mistakes. For the school TV show, I was given a video recorder for creating documentaries. I decided to videotape every party that we had my senior year. I captured ample footage of my friends and me drinking alcohol and using drugs. One day, I accidentally left the tape in the VCR in the school editing room and Mr. Johns found it. Every person I recorded was busted, including top athletes and academic stars. Many were kicked off their sports teams and booted out of their other activities. It was a horrible development and not great for my popularity. I had to apologize to every single person who I essentially ratted out. The captain of the football team was the worst.

"I'm sorry, man. It was an accident."

"I was supposed to go to college on a football scholarship."

I didn't comprehend the magnitude of my error. It never occurred to me that I might be ruining other people's lives. It seemed to all work out for everyone in the end, but I carried around a lot of guilt about the episode. I wasn't willing to face it. Instead, I got as drunk as I possibly could the next weekend. I ran away from the guilt I felt just like I ran away from my anger and sadness.

After Mr. Johns found the tape, he pulled me aside and said, "I want you to know I think you're one of the best leaders at this school. You're a good executive producer. You have a lot going for you, but outside of school, your life is absolute chaos. You need to get it together. No more parties. I want you to learn from this, so I'm taking away your producer position."

I just looked at him and I said, "Okay." I did experience a lot of guilt and shame as a result of my actions, but I truly didn't care what happened to me anymore. As far as I was concerned, partying with my friends was the only important thing in life. It was all a game to me.

The principals talked to me too. One of them said, "You've got everything going for you. You can go to college. You can do anything you want to do."

My response was, "I don't care." I only cared about drinking.

I kept pretending like things were okay on the outside. I dressed well. I took care of myself. But everything on the inside felt like it was dying. I still felt like a wreck. I compared the way my friends appeared with the way I felt on the inside. I wanted to feel the way they looked—happy and confident. Instead, I was moody and on a constant emotional roller coaster ride. I experienced tidal waves of anger and a sadness that approached depression. The only time I felt okay was when I listened to music. I hung out alone in my room doing just that whenever I had a chance. I spent a lot of time trying to impress my friends, but on the inside, I was still the small child who preferred playing in the dark closet by himself.

I don't remember exactly when I started doing drugs, but marijuana was the next thing that came into the picture after alcohol. I resisted smoking weed at first. When I saw my friends do it, they changed into people I didn't want to be. They suddenly looked like stoners who couldn't get things done. They became lazy as hell. I was good at getting things done and I wanted to stay that way because I was helping support my family. I had a lot of weight on my shoulders. I didn't want to lose my drive. I was drinking often and hard, but still able to maintain my edge. I was too intense and I felt too much pressure. When I started smoking pot, it took the edge off and I was able to relax. It was the same kind of relaxation I felt when I first started drinking. I liked drugs in a way that I never liked alcohol. Drinking was never enjoyable, only necessary for escape. I enjoyed drugs and they helped me chill out. Being high felt like a breath of fresh air.

After my sophomore year, I began drinking much harder. My junior and senior years of high school were filled with continuous partying. I hosted many of the parties at my house because Mom was never around. She knew we drank at the house, but she didn't seem to care. Sometimes the neighbors complained and the cops would arrive to bust up the party. Usually we would just move the party to another house. It was my senior year when we got busted at Scott's house. The cops had decided to start cracking down heavily on our nonstop partying.

Michael and Brian got arrested that day. Scott managed to avoid it. Even though I successfully evaded the police, my friends ratted me out at the police station. I woke to my cell phone ringing on Saturday morning.

"This is Sergeant Cody."

"Why are you calling me?"

"I saw you drinking beer yesterday."

"I don't know what you're talking about."

"Taylor, I saw you with my own eyes. You were drinking at Michael's house. Then you were holding beer outside Scott's house. Michael has confirmed you were there."

"I'm sorry, officer. I still don't know what you're talking about."

"You've already been identified by two people. What you're telling me is bullshit. You broke the law. You need to come clean. We need to see you at the station. You're going to be charged with underage possession and consumption."

"Do I really need to come in?"

"Yes. Yes, you do."

I was frantic. I'd never really faced any consequences for my drinking. I had a few previous interactions with the police, but I always got off with a slap on the wrist. I feared this time would be different. I called a lawyer, my friend's dad, who advised me to go to the police station and turn myself in. *Shit. What will I tell Mom and Dad? There's no getting out of this.*

When I arrived, Sergeant Cody was waiting for me. I realized he was the cop I saw getting out of the Infiniti at Scott's house. He had been following us all day, waiting to bust us. *That's just wrong. What we did was no big deal.* I felt violated. I soon learned that Sergeant Cody was no ordinary cop. He was an intelligence officer for the National Guard. He was trying to infiltrate a drug ring that was selling to high school students. Sergeant Cody knew that my friends and I had connections to it and that he could use our underage drinking to extract information from us. He told Michael, Brian, and me that he would give us leniency in exchange for information about the drug dealers. It was either that or be sentenced to one hundred hours of community service. *Why would I do a hundred hours of community service for this fucking community when I can just give the cops some information?* I agreed to the deal.

I nervously bit my nails when I walked into the interrogation room. I sat at a table behind a one-way glass window and answered Sergeant Cody's questions. I didn't give him a lot of information, just the bare minimum. It seemed like a fair trade for my crime, which, in my opinion, wasn't very serious. I walked out of the police station and breathed a sigh of relief. I escaped punishment and I didn't even have to call my parents.

It was difficult to convince me to rat out other people, but I did it to save my own ass. I couldn't accept the consequences of my actions. The punishment I was facing wasn't even that harsh. I had been arrested before, so I knew it wasn't a big deal. Sergeant Cody convinced me it was a bigger deal that time so I would willingly participate in his plan to bust the drug ring. I didn't want to own up to my behavior. I was having fun and I intended to continue turning my life into one constant party.

When I first started getting into trouble with the police, I always got off because Dad would stand up and vouch for me in court. "My son's a good kid. He gets a 4.0." He was able to convince the judge that I shouldn't suffer any consequences. I was arrested seven times before I graduated from high school. Once for theft, once for drug paraphernalia, once for drug possession, twice for underage possession of alcohol, and twice for underage consumption of alcohol. No one believed that I was a good kid anymore. The cops were able to use my endless troublemaking to their advantage and get the information they needed.

My three friends and I were nothing but trouble and the cops knew it. We simply didn't give a shit about anything. Once we started drinking, we did whatever we wanted. We egged people's houses. We crashed other people's parties. We found kids whose parents were going out of town and planned parties at their houses. Even if someone said no, we told everyone to show up at the house anyway. We had no qualms about drinking and driving. There was not one conscience among us. I hung out with those guys continuously, and I was the one who instigated most of the bad behavior. I wasn't alone anymore. I was the leader of the group.

The DEA agent goes over the protocol once more as he finishes attaching the wire to my t-shirt. I feel like I'm in a movie, except all the mob movies I've seen got it wrong. They don't tape the wire to your skin. Who knew? I wish I didn't.

"We've got thirty-five people around the building. One looks like an electrician. One looks like a street cleaner. One is walking the dog. You won't know who they are, but you'll be surrounded by undercover officers at all times. They're there for your safety."

Fucking A. What the hell is going on? How did I get here? Goddamnit! I'm scared out of my mind. "I don't know if I can do this," I say.

He gives me a pep talk. Convinces me that I can do it. That I have to do it.

"Stay calm. Focus on your breath the entire time. You have to breathe or you'll pass out and they'll find the wire."

I pull on my black leather jacket over my wired shirt, and my fingers tremble as I struggle with the zipper. I drive to the house knowing the agents are trailing me and keeping *their eyes on my every move. I'm carrying fifteen hundred dollars in marked bills. I see the street cleaner when I pull up to the house. I make some guesses about who the other undercover officers are among the people I see. I stare at the door, wondering if I can persuade my legs to carry me there. It feels like my feet are cemented to the floor of my car.*

Somehow, I make it inside. How did I get here? How the fuck did I get here? Chill out. Breathe. Make friends with them. It's a sales meeting. Win them over. Get them to trust you. I walk over to the guy in the corner and introduce myself. I have to get him to say his name on tape. He says it. Thank God. One requirement checked off the list. But this is not even close to being over yet.

I'm buying one hundred hits of Ecstasy. I have to count the pills and get him to count the pills. Then I have to count the money and get him to count the money too. The cops have to hear all of it. I begin counting. One, two, three…these feel like the most difficult words I have ever spoken. I get to forty-seven when the guy notices I'm too rattled to count the rest of the pills. He pulls out his revolver and lays it on the table. Shit is getting real now. So real.

I pick up the gun, hold it in the air to examine it, and say, "Cool, man." I know a lot about guns and this one is definitely loaded. I've never been so nervous in my entire life. All my energy is devoted to breathing and preventing my hands from trembling. My insides are quivering though. I can feel my liver shaking. Adrenalin is surging through my body. I set the gun down on the other side of the table, out of his reach. At least I'll have a little bit of time if he goes for it. I'll know the shot is coming.

I finish counting the pills. He counts the pills. Another guy takes over for the money count. We complete the exchange. I've checked everything off the list. I head for the door as quickly as possible.

I hop in my car and drive away. Within minutes, I see flashing lights and I pull over. I'm surrounded by DEA agents. They don't trust me with the drugs. I get out of the car.

"Give me the pills." I hand an agent the bottle and he immediately counts the pills again.

"Good job. We'll be in touch."

It's over. I drive home and get totally wasted.

CHAPTER 3

UNDERCOVER

High school was over but my wild behavior was not. I was no longer a kid who got into some trouble. I was a criminal. At nineteen, I was still living with Mom and partying nonstop. I did the most dangerous thing I could have done; I bought a motorcycle. It was an orange Honda CBR F4i crotch rocket. I called it the Halloween bike.

It was September 20, 2000, and I had tickets to the inaugural Columbus Blue Jackets game. I invited Megan, who was way out of my league, to join me. That afternoon, I donned my black Kevlar jacket, gloves, and helmet with a mirrored face and fin on top before setting out for a ride. My attitude matched my attire. I felt invincible and like I had nothing to lose. I wanted to drive fast, so I did. I drove seventy down a quiet suburban road nestled between two golf courses. The speed limit was thirty-five miles per hour. No one else was on the road, so I didn't believe I was doing anything dangerous.

I arrived at a familiar curve in the road and began leaning into the turn. Suddenly, my left eye locked onto someone hiding between some evergreen trees in the median. *It's a fucking cop!* She was pointing her laser directly at me. There was no way I could brake and maintain control of the bike. I knew I might plow into the officer if I tried. I released the throttle to slow down as I took the turn. That's all I could do. Her partner was sitting in a police car parked just down the road, and she radioed him to pull me over for speeding.

I saw the car's lights turn on. *Fuck that.* I gunned it and passed the cop at one hundred miles per hour. He floored it too, but I knew it was impossible for his car to keep up with my motorcycle. I continued to flee and lost the cop. He obviously called for help because a few minutes later, I spotted another cop car behind me. I sped up to one-fifty and blew through a stop sign. I later learned that two cars almost collided when they swerved to avoid hitting me.

I lost all of the cops and continued driving until I reached the country. I drove my motorcycle into a cornfield and hid. I called Scott and asked him to pick me up so we could load my bike into the back of his truck and take it home.

"Dude, I'm at work right now. I can't pick you up."

"I need your truck. If I go back into town they're going to arrest me, guaranteed."

"I can't leave work. Just find a back road and hope you don't get caught."

"That doesn't sound like a good fucking solution at all."

An hour-and-a-half passed and I started getting nervous about missing my date with Megan. I still needed to go home and shower before picking her up. *Shit. I have to get going. Maybe they forgot about me. It's probably no big deal.* I decided to take off my jacket and leave it in the cornfield. I thought that if I got pulled over wearing a different shirt, I could convince the cops that someone else had been riding my motorcycle.

I drove away, and as soon as I hit one of the main roads, I was pulled over by Delaware County sheriffs. Seven of them were waiting for me in a fast food parking lot. They surrounded me with their guns pulled. It was terrifying. My invincibility came crashing down around me.

"Take the motherfucking keys out of the ignition right now!"

I took the keys out and threw them on the ground.

"Get off the bike and lay face down!"

Fuck. I laid down on the concrete and they smashed my face into the ground. They handcuffed me and threw me into the back of the cruiser. I waited there until the Dublin cops arrived and took me to the police station.

On the drive over, one of the cops said, "Sergeant Cody is waiting for you."

"Why?"

"He wants to talk to you."

Unbelievable. Sergeant Cody was trying to go places. He needed people like me to get into trouble so he could extract information from us. I saw him as soon as I walked into the station. They booked me, confiscated my things, set bond, and led me into a holding cell.

Cody eventually came in and said, "Hunt, I wondered if I would see you again. You have to bail yourself out today, but I can give you some leniency if you help us one more time." He explained that I was being charged with speeding in addition to a felony count of fleeing and alluding and a felony count of reckless operation. *Two felonies? Shit! All I wanted was to go fast on my motorcycle.* I still thought of myself as a good kid from a good home, despite the reality of my behavior. I wasn't willing to face felony penalties. I knew I would have to hire a lawyer and spend a large amount of money to have the charges reduced.

I'm sure Sergeant Cody knew exactly what was going through my head. He was a smooth talker. "Just tell us what you know. This time, you're going to have to give us the good stuff because what you gave us last time was bullshit." He told me I could think about it and he would be in touch. I bailed myself out and actually made it to the game with Megan. I couldn't pay attention to her though. All I could think about was the choice I had in front of me. I either had to face some serious consequences or rat out more people. I felt enormous dread.

A few days later, Sergeant Cody called. When I met him in a library parking lot, he explained the deal to me. "You're facing two felonies and six months in jail for each one. To get out of the charges, you're going to have to buy from the dealers this time. The DEA will be involved. The people you've been buying from are running a much bigger operation than you realize."

My drug use was escalating, and I had just recently started doing cocaine. I had connections to the dealers that went back to my high school days and Cody knew that. I couldn't face the idea of jail time and I didn't want to pay a fortune in legal fees, so I agreed to the deal. I had no idea what lay ahead of me. When I walked into the DEA office for the first time and saw the photo of President Clinton, I immediately knew I had gotten myself into something that was much more serious than my high school snitching. I worked with the DEA agents for a few months before having to wear the wire while purchasing the pills. I didn't realize that was part of the deal in the beginning. Instead, the agents slowly introduced the plan, only giving me the information I needed to know at each stage. By the time I found out about the wire, I was in too deep to back out.

It was about a week before I wore the wire when they told me I would have to do it. *No way. I was just trying to weasel my way out of serious trouble. I didn't agree to this.* My apprehension was apparent.

"Listen, the prosecutor isn't convinced he should drop the charges. You've got quite a record. But if you wear this wire and get the hundred pills for us, we think we can persuade him to cut you a deal."

I knew I was being manipulated, but they had all the power. The pressure I felt to avoid the charges was great enough to convince me that I had to do it. The night I wore the wire was the scariest night of my life. I was convinced the dealers were going to find the wire and kill me. After I made it out alive, the weight of what had happened drove me to heavier drinking and using. I couldn't deal with the reality of my life. I needed to escape.

When I went to the courthouse after my role in the bust was over, the prosecutor said, "I've dropped all of your charges. Thanks for helping us out." I was relieved, but I walked away wondering if the dealers were going to find out what I had done and kill me. I realized I had traded my sense of safety for the opportunity to escape punishment for my crimes. I didn't care about the people I exposed, but I still felt bad about what I had done. My life was chaos, and I wasn't responsible enough to pay the consequences for my actions. I felt like a coward and that made me even more volatile. I was emotionally all over the place. To hide that, I chose to use even more.

———

Scott and I are drinking at my apartment and decide to start bar hopping. Sundays are not good for this. None of our favorite bars are open. I never drink on Sundays. I might take some pills, but Sunday is my day of rest from drinking. I do still have standards.

Hours pass and we are getting wasted. Nonstop drinking and driving from place to place. We're bored with our options, so we decide to move from a bar in the city to a bar in the suburb, closer to home. We aren't worried about the drive because everyone knows there are no cops out on Sunday. No one gets drunk on Sunday. The more we drink, the more courageous we get. We just don't care anymore. The fifteen-minute drive down the freeway takes us twelve.

The pub is slow on a Sunday night. We shut the place down. I make a right turn out of the parking lot to take us home. Scott turns up the techno music as my foot rests heavily on the gas pedal. We're dancing in the car and having fun. For a brief period of time, we're invincible.

The cop car whips back around after we pass it and I see lights in my rear view mirror. "Fuck." The dark tinted windows of my Eclipse have gotten the officer's attention. Or *maybe it's the speeding and swerving. We both quickly put on our seatbelts and I throw a bunch of mints in my mouth. Scott checks his pockets for anything that could get him in trouble. He realizes what's about to happen to me and makes a call from his cell phone.*

I get out of the car. They're shining lights in my face. "Stand on one foot. Arms out like a T. Count backwards from one hundred."

"Who can do this stuff sober?" They're toying with me. I'm pissed because they're making a show out of this. I refuse to blow. Holy shit, I know I'm in trouble.

"We have enough information to arrest you." Scott's brother picks him up from the side of the road as I get in the cop car. The tow truck is on the way for my car.

At the station, they ask me, "Do you want anyone to come pick you up?"

"No, I don't remember anyone's number." The only number I know is Dad's, and I refuse to call him.

"We're going to hold you until you can post bail."

"I can post my own bail. I have the money."

"Someone else has to bail you out."

They ask for my shoelaces and belt so I can't hang myself. I'm beyond angry as I sit on the metal bed in the white concrete cell. I know I'm going to have to face the consequences. Through the glass I say, "I don't want anyone to pick me up. There's no one to pick me up."

In the morning, they won't release me because I'm still drunk. Donna, my dad's wife, comes to pick me up. "What happened?" she asks.

The guilt, shame, and remorse suddenly return. They are the same exact feelings I had when I woke up with my head in the pot and Mom screaming over me. Getting a DUI was one of those things I was never going to end up doing. I did it. I've violated my own code of conduct.

CHAPTER 4

SHATTERED ILLUSION

I started doing sales for Dad's produce company right out of high school. Even though I was still angry with Dad, I was enticed by the potential to make a lot of money working for him. I knew that more money meant more partying for me. *You're going to pay me how much? Hell yeah, I'll work for you!* I was highly successful, but selling was never a comfortable job for me. I was still the socially awkward teenager I had been in high school. I preferred being a loner, and working in sales pushed me far outside my comfort zone. I hated approaching people I didn't know and making small talk. It seemed like bullshit to me. It made me feel vulnerable, and I was extremely uncomfortable with vulnerability. That uneasiness turned up the volume on my character flaws. I couldn't sell by being truthful and real with people. Instead, I was dishonest and manipulative in my tactics—a stereotypical sleazy salesman.

I hated myself for it, just like I had hated myself from a very young age. It started around age eight. *Why do*

I look like this? I'm too skinny. My freckles are ugly. Why don't I look different? I never felt like I fit the mold, and I disliked absolutely everything about myself. My head was still constantly filled with that kind of negative self-talk. I didn't like who I was, but I didn't know who I should be instead. *Who am I? What am I here to do? This is not how my life should look.* I knew things weren't right, and that disconnect produced a perpetual storm in my mind. I was angry, impulsive, and volatile. I couldn't stand the person I was. Because I didn't like my true self, I was a chameleon who changed myself to fit in with the people around me at any given moment. Who I was on the inside never matched the personality I projected on the outside.

I needed alcohol and drugs to escape the storm and the discomfort of my sales job. Between the ages of eighteen and twenty-three, I went to work drunk or high most days. It helped with the awkwardness, at first. Approaching a potential customer while sober made me very anxious. I worried I would have nothing to say, so I rehearsed conversations in my head before meetings. Drinking took the edge off and diminished my social awkwardness. For about two years, alcohol allowed me to become an extrovert for a couple of hours so I could close deals.

I sweated profusely during all of my sales meetings. It was chemically induced, not natural, sweatiness. My slippery palms during handshakes were the perfect mirrors of my character. Many people wanted nothing to do with me because they sensed that something was not right. But somehow, I still managed to sell big deals during rare lucid moments. I made close to a million dollars during those five years, but I had nothing to show for it. I spent all of my money on drugs, alcohol, and a bunch of stupid shit.

After a few years, I was drinking and using so much that the alcohol and drugs became a hindrance. I could no longer carry on a coherent conversation with a customer. I remember walking into a Chinese restaurant and attempting to sell our produce while drunk and high. I was so high that I couldn't understand anything the owner said. Nor could I say anything that was comprehensible to her. I simply couldn't put together a sentence. There was no way I was getting that woman's business because she could see I was unstable. That scene was repeated many times. Any time I failed at getting a sale, I began questioning my abilities and lost my confidence. Then I would spend all weekend on a cocaine binge.

My partying had transformed into full-blown addiction. My drinking and using was out of control. I took so many drugs that my body was confused and constantly buzzing. I rarely ate any food. I managed to remain employed despite never showing up on time and frequently nodding off at my desk. When I was at the office, I spent most of my time searching for ways to buy drugs. I had an expense account, which was a dangerous thing. I went to bars every night, drank massive amounts of alcohol, and bought it for other people. It was the only way I knew how to make friends. Just like in high school, I still lacked interpersonal skills and partying was my only doorway into social life. Anytime I was not out partying, my behavior was reclusive and I stayed home by myself. I still spent a lot of time alone in my room, but instead of just listening to music, I was also drinking and taking drugs. I took more with each passing day, and that was bringing me closer to the point of death.

On one hand, my relationship with Dad was great because I was selling so much. But on the other hand, we had some conflict because everyone at work was questioning my behavior. They would tell Dad, "You need to talk to your son. Something is wrong with him." They could see that I was slurring my words and passing out. My mind was cloudy. I might be in the office physically, but I was not really present. My coworkers wondered how I was selling anything at all. I only continued to succeed at sales because I had periodic spurts of extreme productivity. They only occurred when I felt really pressured. I would get high and then see one hundred customers in two days. I would close some big deals and then the pressure would be off, so I would go back to doing nothing for a while. I repeated that cycle over and over.

Dad never initiated a conversation with me about my drinking and using. Instead, he told me I was getting a promotion since I was doing so well. The company named me Vice President of Sales. I accepted the position because it came with a higher salary, even though I wasn't interested in taking on more responsibility or doing the extra work that was required. I wanted to spend even more of my time getting high, and more money would allow me to do just that.

Promoting me was a bad decision because I wasn't able to control myself, much less manage other people. Dad knew I had the attributes of a strong leader, but I wasn't able to manifest them because I was lost in my addiction. I was tasked with training and mentoring the other sales reps at the same time I was unraveling. I refused to admit that I wasn't the right person for the job though. Having six employees report to me further inflated my already huge ego. But, despite my problems, giving me the job was good for business. The promotion reenergized me and made me focus on work again. Sales improved, but that was short lived.

My coworkers continued to judge me harshly, but there was no one else in my life to even question my lifestyle. The people I spent time with outside of work were drinking and using too, so my behavior was not disturbing to them. I tried to avoid my family as much as possible. I didn't spend time with Dad outside of work. Even though Amber sometimes partied with me, she didn't know the magnitude of my problem. Amanda never saw that side of me, so she assumed I was fine. I was still doing some things to take care of Mom. I was the one who always asked her if she was okay. Mom understood that it was off limits to ask me the same question because I did my best to convince her and everyone else that I was doing fine. I went to great lengths to maintain the deception and hide the truth that my life was in turmoil.

Getting a DUI was significant because it was impossible to hide. My carefully constructed illusion was shattered. It suddenly became more difficult for me to convince others that I had it all together. I felt like I was publically shamed and there was a black mark on my legal record. It was the first time I had to fully accept the consequences of my dangerous behavior. I knew I was in real and inescapable trouble. My license was revoked immediately. I had to ask Dad to pick me up for work each day, and that was humiliating. My coworkers' suspicions were confirmed.

I spent seven thousand dollars trying unsuccessfully to get out of the DUI charge. I wasn't offered a deal. I couldn't escape punishment by ratting out someone else like I had before. I was treated like the criminal I really was.

My feelings of guilt, shame, and remorse reached new heights. I needed more drugs and I needed them fast. Conveniently, my workplace was in a rough neighborhood, and some of my coworkers sold drugs. I started soliciting from them without even knowing for sure they could get me what I wanted. One day I said to a guy named Bob, "Hey, I got a DUI. I've been drinking too much and I was wondering if you can get me some painkillers to take instead." It turned out that Bob was the right person to ask. He gave me forty Percocets in exchange for forty dollars.

My coworkers' respect for me fell even further, and some of them began questioning me face to face. They never kindly asked, "Are you okay?" Instead, they said things like, "What the hell is wrong with you? You're slurring your words and nodding off. Nothing you say makes sense. We think you have a fucking drug problem."

I felt cornered and attacked when they questioned me, so I responded in fits of rage. "I don't have a fucking drug problem! I'm the number one sales rep! When you learn to sell something, you can talk to me about my life. Until then, you can go fuck yourself!" I was becoming a monster.

As far as I was concerned everyone else needed to mind their own business. I convinced myself I was doing great and I was happy to pat myself on the back. The words that came out of my mouth were pointed and vile.

On the rare occasions that Dad questioned my behavior, I lashed out at him just as violently. Screaming at him, I said, "You cheated on Mom and you're not even in my life anymore! Who the fuck do you think you're talking to? I'm your best sales rep! I dare you to fire me! What would you do without me?"

No one wanted to deal with that kind of response from me, even though it was becoming clearer that I had a major problem. I didn't have someone in my life who was strong enough to call me out and say, "You're full of shit. You have a drug problem and you need to get help." My coworkers didn't approach me in a way that would deflate me. They wanted a battle with me, and I was always determined to win.

I felt so threatened by my coworkers' attacks because I couldn't picture my life without drugs and alcohol. Drinking and using was the only way I had to deal with my problems and make it through life. I saw no other options, so the threat of it being taken away was utterly terrifying to me. I had to win the battle to keep my drugs. *If you take them away from me, I'm going to have to face my past. I'm not willing to feel the pain. I won't cry.* My drinking and using seemed like a friend at first because it helped me cope. Even though it had quickly morphed into an enemy, I was still protecting it. I needed it. I couldn't let it go. I would have nothing. It was my only friend.

Although I wasn't ready to face my unresolved issues and change my life, I sometimes had moments of clarity when I woke up after partying hard the night before. There was a voice in my head that clearly knew the difference between right and wrong. *You're supposed to be living a richer life. This is shallow. There is a different way.*

Find it. The voice was a blessing, but I didn't know how to heed its advice. I tried to figure it out by writing in my journal and writing poems. The questions I asked were always the same. *What is the voice? How can I do what it's telling me? Where is the escape from this life of drama and carnage that I've created?* I had no answers. I had no tools to help me escape. My problem felt ugly, dark, deep, and lonely. I was filled with despair.

Now that I have work privileges, I'm driving myself home and no longer have to listen to Dad giving me a hard time about how my life is going. He is so disappointed in me and he let me know about it every single day on the drive home from work. It was like getting beaten down over and over again, like having the worst Groundhog Day possible. In the car today, it's my own mind beating me down instead of Dad.

You aren't good enough. Look what you've become. This is how you are always going to be. You aren't any good. You should have listened to your doubts from the very beginning because what you're doing and how you're living is not okay. You've just proven that you're not good enough through your actions. So much doom and gloom in my head.

It's mental anguish and I can only take so much of it. I need an out. I'm so close to home, but instead of continuing to drive, I turn into the liquor store, walk inside, and buy a fifth of whiskey. This will help.

My apartment is empty when I enter. It's Friday and no one I know wants to hang out. My roommate is still at work. This is the first place I've lived since moving out of

Mom's house and it's not impressive. The windows are covered with cheap plastic blinds and my mattress lies on the floor of my bedroom covered in shitty old cotton sheets. I grab a knife from the drawer and lay it on the kitchen table next to the whiskey. I walk into my bedroom to find a piece of paper and a pen, return to the kitchen, then sit and stare at the spiders crawling across the vinyl floor as I drink from the bottle. I start covering the white paper with blue ink, writing a letter to my family.

I'm crying, drinking, and I'm writing a list of all of the regrets and unresolved issues I have with each person. I feel so much guilt and shame. There's too much pain. I'm going to kill myself. It's over. Things would be much better without me. I can't take this struggle anymore. I don't have any way out. What is life supposed to look like? I just don't know.

My tears are smearing the ink. I drink more. I write the bad things I've done and say sorry for things I don't even need to be sorry for. I write the things I'm angry about. I ask them to forgive me for what I'm about to do. So much anger. So much sadness. So fucking sad.

I'm trying to cut my wrist with the knife. It's probably better if I do this in my room. I want to die on my bed. I carry the letter, the bottle, and the knife upstairs. I finish the letter at my desk and then place it face down inside my brown mole-skinned journal. I'm signing off. I'm a disgrace. I can't get my shit together. Look what I've done to my family. Inside, I'm standing at the edge of the really deep *sadness. It's been there from the beginning. A gaping, God-sized hole.*

Standing at the edge of my mattress, I know for the first time that not only is something fundamentally wrong with me, but there is also something missing. Something huge. It's created a gaping sadness in me. I am so ashamed. Guilt and shame are layered on top of anxiety. I'm supposed to be living a different life, but I don't know how. Dying is the only solution. The dull knife makes slow progress across my wrist. Finally, it's enough and there's blood. Lots of blood.

The room is spinning. I fall back into the soft abyss of my bed and take the last few gulps of whiskey. Staring up at the ceiling, I know everything is gone. Game over. I drift off on a wave of blood and alcohol, sickness and sadness.

CHAPTER 5

TOO MUCH PAIN

I was bleeding pretty badly when I went to sleep, so I was convinced I would not be waking up. But I awoke to find the inside of my wrist stuck to the bottom sheet. I must have laid my wrist on the sheet just perfectly. It had sealed my wound shut. I looked at the dried blood on the white cotton sheet in disbelief. I felt like a complete failure. *What do I do now?*

I realized I needed to go to work but had no idea how I was going to face anyone after what I had just done. I was not relieved to be alive. I was disappointed. The pain I felt was even greater than the pain that had driven me to suicide. A gulf of emptiness opened up inside of me as I slowly peeled the sheet from my arm. It was a void made of confusion. I lacked answers and I lacked direction. All I had was sadness. In the midst of the sorrow, I managed to bandage my arm and drive myself to work.

When I saw Dad, I didn't tell him what had happened. I didn't tell anyone. My suicide attempt wasn't a ploy for attention. I truly didn't want to live anymore. I sat next to my coworkers all day without speaking to anyone. Even though I was not physically alone at the office, my emotional solitude was absolute, and my sadness was unbearable. Each day, I went to work and stared at a computer screen for eight hours. Then I drove home, got drunk or high, and went to sleep. I woke up and did the exact same thing the next day. *Why can't I stop?* Weeks passed and I felt like I was in purgatory. It was an empty existence. I had a lot of material stuff, but I had nothing at all of real value in my life. My outward appearance was merely a façade. Nothing felt dear to me. I had no love for anyone. I was disconnected from my family and everyone else. Only one person even bothered to ask why I had a bandage around my wrist. A driver at work named Reggie looked at me and asked, "What's wrong with your wrist, man? Why is there blood on your bandage? What's going on with you?"

"I cut myself."

"Oh really? You cut yourself?"

"Yes, I cut myself on accident," I said, without realizing he could see right through me. Reggie was one of the first recovering addicts with whom I had contact. He could sense what was really going on with me. Some recovering alcoholics and addicts just know, I would later learn. Today, I can tell you the instant I meet someone if they share my affliction. I can feel the mark on a fellow addict's soul.

Reggie was the only one who noticed because I was living in such isolation. I know Dad cared about me, but I couldn't let him in. I was still holding the breakup of our family against him five years after the divorce. My friends knew I had a problem, but no one was close enough to give me the tough love that I needed. I wanted close friends, but didn't know how to be a good friend to others. I never let anyone get to know me. All of my relationships were superficial and distant. I was convinced that if people knew about all of the skeletons hidden in my closet, they wouldn't want to be anywhere near me. *I can't stand to be around myself.* It was painful to see me on my course of destruction.

Slitting my wrist was a cry for change. I wanted to change but I didn't know how. I knew I needed to stop drinking and using but I didn't know what my life would look like without drugs and alcohol. I did know that I would have to face all of my unresolved issues, and that seemed impossible. Sometimes I felt enormous waves of emotion during the brief sober hours of my mornings. They were unbearable and made me feel like crying. But I was uncomfortable with the idea of crying. I couldn't face all of the bad things I had done or the anger I still felt about my parents' divorce. I believed it was more baggage than I could carry. It was too overwhelming. I was too proud to admit that I needed help. I simply couldn't do it.

Failing at suicide felt like failure on top of failure. I was only twenty but I had a century of pain built up inside of me. I wanted to escape. I'm certain I was clinically depressed, even if it was only brought on by all of the drugs I was taking. I crossed the line between sanity and insanity. My emotions made me feel physically ill. My sadness was so deep that my soul was only a flicker of a flame, susceptible to being blown out by the slightest breeze. My life was exceptionally fragile. I was going to die.

The guilt, shame, and remorse from attempting suicide was layered on top of the humiliation I still felt from my DUI. I was doing well in sales and other companies had been attempting to recruit me. I knew I could have a very successful career if I worked hard, but instead I found myself wanting to pull out my hair every time Dad came to pick me up for work. The lectures on the drive each day were fucking terrible. Even when I regained my driving privileges, I felt like a failure. I didn't understand why I couldn't get my life together, solve my alcohol and drug problem, and keep myself out of trouble. At age twenty, my DUI was my eighth arrest. I was clearly failing at life and my ego couldn't accept that. Instead of humbling me and convincing me to seek help, the DUI made me feel angrier, more driven, and more self-important. It was a warning shot fired across the bow of a ship indicating I was headed for more trouble if I didn't change course. Unfortunately, it wasn't a big enough warning shot for me.

My already heavy drinking increased tenfold to deal with the expanding emptiness I felt inside. After I tried to kill myself, I started searching for an explanation for how I got to the point of wanting to end my life. I identified alcohol as the culprit. I believed that heavy drinking drove me to the point of suicide, so I made a conscious decision to stop drinking so much and switch to primarily taking painkillers. Since I was drinking when I attempted suicide, drugs seemed like a safer option. I also didn't want to get another DUI because it cost me so much money. I believed drugs would prevent that as well.

As I pulled away from alcohol, my craving for drugs became intense. My obsession grew and I continually needed more and more. Bob was my reliable source at work, so I continued to buy from him. I was happy because my pill habit made me feel like I had become more responsible. It felt cleaner too. I felt sloppy when I drank, but I wasn't sloppy on painkillers. They didn't give me blurred vision and I could still drive. *I'm the responsible one. The rest of you are sloppy, fucking drunks.* Problem solved. I successfully transformed one addiction into another without even understanding what I had done.

The craving kicks in immediately as I roll out of bed. I took seven pills last night, so I know I have only one left. There's no way I can make it through the entire day on that. I'll get so sick I will feel like dying. I'll have to find more.

I walk into the bathroom and put my last pill in my mouth to dissolve the coating. Then I dry it off with my white shirt, leaving a green tie-dye stain. I place it in the cellophane on the countertop and prepare to crush it. As soon as my lighter touches it, the pill slides out from under the cellophane and right into the drain. Fuck! It's the only one I have. What will I do? I'm devastated.

I panic and say every cuss word I know. I have to get that pill into my system because I'm starting to feel ill. It's the only way I'm going to be okay and make it through the next eight hours. I don't have any more and they're hard to get. Money is getting kind of tight. Each Oxycontin 80 is fifty bucks and I buy eight every day. I'm out of cash.

The craving is overwhelming. I'm frantically trying to come up with a plan to retrieve the pill. I've heard stories about crackheads carpet surfing. I guess I'm going drain diving. I have no choice. I will die if I don't get it. I know I will.

I unscrew the pipes to take the drain apart. Or rather, I rip it apart. The pill is gone and I've got the empty pipes in my hands. In a sudden moment of clarity and sanity, I catch a glimpse of my desperate reflection in the mirror.

What am I doing?

How did I get here?

How did I become this animal?

To the reflection I say, "You're at your house ripping the sink apart to find a pill. It's chaos in here. Normal people don't do these things." For the first time, I know that I have a problem.

CHAPTER 6

OUT OF CONTROL

Mentally, I felt much better on painkillers. Heavy drinking intensified my already depressive tendencies. Pills gave me a euphoric experience and I felt like I was in a renaissance period. I loved life again and believed I was going to be okay. In reality, I wasn't happy, just high. But I didn't know that. I thought the fog had finally lifted. Plus, I considered the pills to be medication. As far as I was concerned, I had medically pulled myself out of depression by drinking less alcohol and taking more pills.

Taking pills was exciting. I got butterflies in my stomach whenever I had pills in my hand that I was getting ready to take. The anticipation thrilled me. I was never excited to drink. Just like when I first smoked pot in high school, I realized that I enjoyed drugs in a way that I had never enjoyed alcohol. I liked that I felt the effects of painkillers more quickly too. They took the edge off within half an hour and things suddenly felt great to me. Alcohol never really took the edge off for me anymore. I simply used it for maintenance, to make it through life the best I could.

I saw myself in a different light once I started relying mostly on painkillers. Again, I viewed a pill habit as a more responsible form of chemical reliance than drinking. I felt sharper and more clearheaded. Obviously, I was no longer a danger to myself or others like I had been while drinking and driving or slitting my wrist. I found renewed confidence at work and felt like I was finally getting my shit together. I considered myself to be pain free for the first time in a long time. Pills don't heal emotional pain though; they only mask it. All of my pain was in my heart, but I couldn't admit that. Instead of resolving my issues, I was only burying them more deeply.

The renaissance period was short lived. My tolerance to painkillers steadily increased and, within a year, I was taking twenty pills each day. Soon, they lost their effectiveness completely and I had to find something stronger. I moved from Vicodin to Percocet, to morphine, and finally to Oxycontin. My desperation intensified each time I progressed to a stronger drug. *This is getting out of control again.* The period of decline that spanned the years between my first drink and my attempted suicide was over. I began a new chapter of deterioration that would lead me into the very depths of darkness. I could not escape the hold painkillers had on me. I was completely dependent. I could no longer live without them. I was addicted.

I used to spend a lot of money on alcohol, but painkillers are much more expensive. I spent four hundred dollars per day on Oxycontin. *This is outrageous. It's unsustainable, but there's no good way out.* I felt pressure to increase my sales at work to support my habit, but that was tough to do because my health was terrible. I wasn't eating right. I was way too skinny. I couldn't go to the bathroom. Simply functioning as a human being was becoming much more difficult, so being productive at work was an even greater stretch. I still worked for Dad's company and he was becoming more concerned. All of my coworkers could see that my life had taken an even sharper turn towards disaster. I was never on time and I couldn't follow a conversation. I could no longer function at work. The painkillers and the behavior surrounding my addiction were the shovel I was using to actively dig my own grave.

Oxycontin 80s were the only pills that were still effective. They were green with an outer coating that I had to remove by putting them in my mouth. Then I crushed and snorted them. They're pretty hardcore, not for the lightweight pill user. Other people I knew took one or two. I took between five and eight each day. They were killing me and I was totally out of it at all times. The desperation I felt led me to a place where I had never been before, a place where I dismantled an entire sink trying to recover one pill.

In that moment when I caught my reflection in the mirror, I understood I was not on the correct path. I felt empty, gray, and gross inside. The only way I could keep the sadness at bay was to take more pills. I was right back at it in the same way I had been drinking before. I knew I was sad, but I couldn't even cry anymore because I was so numb to my sorrows. And I didn't understand why I was sad. My life seemed like a show that I was watching on television. I could see the events that happened from day to day, but I wasn't present for any of them. I knew there had to be another way to live. I just couldn't escape my patterns and find it myself. I needed help.

The first time that became clear to me was after a night of watching basketball with my coworker, Tim. He was one of the sales reps I was mentoring. We drove to Cleveland and sat courtside to see LeBron James play. At the game, we met up with Ray, a sales rep for one the companies we represented. Ray bought the tickets for us and started buying huge beers for Tim and me. We were all having a great time. I decided to turn the fun up a notch and took a bag of Adderall out of my pocket. I offered them to the other guys. Ray declined, Tim took one pill, and I took ten. As I watched LeBron run down the court, I saw Ray shoot me a look of disgust. Normal people don't take ten Adderalls at a basketball game.

I blacked out at the game and only came to when I was dancing at a bar later that night. Again, my eyes met Ray's. He was staring at me. The snapshot of his face illuminated by the red lights in the bar is forever burned in my memory. The look he gave me pierced my being and I knew he could see right through me. Ray understood that I was trouble, and he wasn't the only one. Most people were scared to be around me because they could never predict which Taylor they were going to get. I could be lucid or foggy, kind or vicious. Avoiding me was the safest tactic.

Tim and I spent the night at a hotel in Cleveland and then got on the road back to Columbus in the morning. During the drive home, I began crying and couldn't stop. The emotions I'd been working hard to bury suddenly broke free in a torrential flood. I recognized that I was living the wrong way and didn't want to do it anymore. I didn't know how to stop though. I had never heard about any of the solutions to addiction. I thought overcoming it was all about willpower, and I didn't have enough of that. I stared at Tim from the passenger seat, wondering what to do.

"Man, why are you crying?"

"I need help."

"Let's get you some help then. What's going on?" Tim had no idea how serious my problem was.

"Dude, I've got good stuff going on but I can't stop drinking. I can't stop using. I feel like my life is all fiction. I think I've got a fucking problem."

"What should I do?"

"Call my sister, please."

Tim called Amber and said, "Hey, I've got Taylor in the car. We're driving back from Cleveland and he's asking for help. Should I take him to the hospital?"

Amber told Tim she would meet us at Talbot Hall, a treatment center. I cried for the entire two-hour drive that remained. I knew I had issues but I didn't know why they were coming to a head at that moment. The tears just wouldn't stop.

Amber packed a bag for me and was at Talbot Hall when we arrived. We walked inside and I was asked to complete a drug and alcohol questionnaire. Despite all the pain I felt, I lied when I answered the questions. After Tim called Amber, I spent the rest of the car ride convincing myself I didn't have a problem. By the time we reached the center, I knew I didn't want to be there so I started concocting a story to get myself out of it. I slammed the door shut on my brief moment of honesty.

How many pills do you take? *One.*

How often do you do drugs? *Once per week.*

The lies went on and on, but I still qualified to be admitted once I finished the form. *Dammit. I don't want to be here.* In treatment, I was introduced to the solution to addiction for the first time. My response was far from positive. It all sounded like ridiculous bullshit to me.

My disease was in control and working hard to convince me that I wasn't an addict. It was a pivotal moment because it was the first time I let my guard down enough to admit that something was wrong. But it only lasted a couple of hours before denial took hold again. *I don't have a problem. I just need a few pills.* I couldn't imagine my life without drugs. *I can't let them take that away from me.* My disease was fighting for its life.

When I met Sara in the treatment center, she intrigued me. I was attracted to her darkness because I could relate to it. When I heard the things she was saying about heroin I thought, "Oh, I've never tried that. I need to try it." That was in the back of my head when she gave me her number so we could be sober support for each other when we got out. I text her this afternoon for two reasons. One, because I might want to date her. Two, because I want to find out how serious she is about sobriety and see if she can get heroin for me.

I park my car on the street and look up to see a brick building with shitty windows. It looks like an old public housing project that's been rehabbed. There is no parking lot. Nothing about the place looks nice. I go inside and walk up the two flights of stairs to her apartment. When Sara lets me in, I feel like I enter a shell of an apartment. It's small with a couch that looks like it was picked up from the curb. The yellow and red plaid looks like something straight out of the seventies. There is a sterile feel, like she is just occupying space instead of actually living here. It's not a home.

Sara seems weird. When she talks, her sentences are incomplete and her thoughts are incoherent. I have to pay really close attention to make any sense out of what she says. She is in and out of it, too scattered to hold a conversation together. She's high. It's the first time I've seen her high. Her face is pale and she's wearing too much makeup. She looks like a zombie.

"Are you shooting up?"

"Yes." She shows me a broken needle stuck in her forearm.

"How did that happen?"

"The needle broke off in my arm. It will have to be surgically removed."

It's gross and it's ridiculous, but I'm intrigued.

"You want to get high?"

"I've never done it before. Fuck it," I say. This is one of the worst phrases for me as an addict to say because it means I've just given up on sobriety. She's high and I want to be high. "You stick the needle in my arm. I'll turn my head."

Sara's been doing black tar heroin. It's sticky, nasty stuff that's impossible to get off your fingers. She puts some in a spoon, adds water, and heats it with a lighter until it dissolves into a soupy paste. Then she drops a cotton filter into the mixture and it puffs up like a sponge. She draws the heroin into a syringe while I roll up my sleeve and give her my arm. Sara tightens a belt around my arm like a *tourniquet and I suddenly feel butterflies in my stomach. What am I doing? I should back out before it's too late.*

But I don't. I can't. I turn my head and look the other way while she sticks me with the needle. It's uncomfortable, but then the heroin enters in my bloodstream and I feel the effects in a few seconds. I feel a wave of heat throughout my body. Then I feel the endorphin rush. I feel calm, but the room is spinning. I'm so relaxed I sink into the couch and close my eyes. This feeling resonates with me. I feel good. I feel great. I want more.

I open my eyes. "Do that again."

Sara shoots me up a second time and a black haze arrives. My vision is closing in. Everything shuts down. I'm falling.

CHAPTER 7

FLATLINED

Being admitted into Talbot Hall was the beginning of the end of my using. Unfortunately, the end was still very far away. In treatment, I learned about the twelve steps of recovery. They didn't make a lot of sense to me. Some were about God and others were about taking inventory and making amends. *An inventory of what?* I was told that meetings were an important part of recovery. *Meetings? I don't want to go to any goddamn meetings. I've got better things to do.* I was dismissive of the entire program. My life was shit and I couldn't understand how meetings were going to make it any better. *Obviously you people don't understand my problem.* I didn't think a treatment center was the right place for me to be.

It was bizarre there. My life outside that had been complete chaos suddenly became completely regimented when I was admitted. There was a time for everything. "You get fifteen minutes of television and you can only watch channel twenty-eight." *Are you kidding me? This is stupid.* Smoking breaks and mealtimes were scheduled. I was required to talk to doctors and to attend classes and meetings. It felt like jail. We were herded like cattle from room to room. "Now you have fifteen minutes of alone time." There was a constant train of events. I was used to just getting high and zonking out on my couch in front of the television all the time. Most of us were. *I don't want to do this shit. I just want to fucking relax.* What I really wanted to do was go home and get high.

I wanted to get high even more urgently once the drugs were out of my system and I started to feel all of my suppressed emotions. Allowing myself to feel all of my anger and sadness was new to me and it felt terrible. I was desperate to escape the pain. I wasn't convinced that I wanted to get sober, so I looked for excuses not to do it. In treatment, they told me about a design for living. I didn't think it was the correct design for me. I thought I should be able to choose a different one for myself. They told me I had to follow the guidelines or I would slip up. They called them suggestions, but they weren't really suggestions. I thought they felt like wearing a straightjacket. At meetings, people hugged each other when they met. I was so disconnected from other human beings that I didn't want to be hugged. *Don't touch me. I don't need to be touched, especially not by you.* The other people were a bunch of crackheads and I thought I was above that. I never did the serious things they did. I just had a slight pill problem.

I was still a loner and didn't want to be a part of any group. Throughout my entire life, I felt like I was on the outside looking in. I never fit in, so I became fiercely independent. In treatment, I learned that the first step of recovery is, "We admitted we were powerless over alcohol." *We* not *I.* It's a group thing. Addiction is all about

I. I needed to get more drugs to survive. As part of treatment, I had to go to meetings and take part in group counseling sessions. They were trying to reintegrate me into society. Addicts don't usually have many friends. We don't get along with others. We push people away. We're angry and judgmental. Our lives are devastating for ourselves and for others. In recovery, we have to start talking to one another. I had to be honest with others and hear feedback about myself that was uncomfortable. I wasn't ready to do that yet. I was still satisfied to hang out in the dark closet by myself with my addiction.

At Talbot Hall, I was told to make friends, go to meetings, and work the steps as a design for living. I ignored all of it except the part about making friends. What I didn't hear was that I was supposed to make friends with people I met at meetings who were sober and serious about living differently. Instead, I made friends with other drug addicts in the treatment center who, like me, were not really interested in getting sober. I went from being a solitary drug addict to having a group of friends who were also addicts. We exchanged contact information so we could get together after treatment. That was a disaster. After I left Talbot Hall, I only stayed sober for three weeks.

A group of us got out of treatment at the same time and ended up getting high together one night. My new friends introduced me to heroin, and needles entered the picture for the first time. Before treatment, I'd only been taking painkillers. As my disease progressed, I became willing to do things I swore that I would never do. I drew a line in the sand that I wouldn't cross, but I kept moving that line out of desperation. Eventually, I'd do anything to get high. Sara was a heroin addict I met at Talbot Hall who was completely lost. She was unhinged and I kind of liked that about her. Sara was definitely not trying to get sober, and neither was I. When I let her shoot me up for the first time, I was craving drugs so much that I was willing to do something I had never done before.

I flatlined.

The initial hit of heroin gave me a craving that kicked in instantly. I wanted to do it again. After the second hit, I turned blue and blacked out. I woke up with a pounding headache amidst a fury of chaos, wondering what happened. All of my joints hurt and I didn't feel like I could move. Two paramedics were standing over me yelling. I saw wires extending from white pads attached to my chest. A feeling of dread washed over me. *What the fuck just happened? Why are they so close to me? Why are they yelling?* There was extreme commotion as the paramedics stomped around the apartment. I couldn't shake the pulsating feeling that was traveling throughout my body. My head was spinning.

I later found out that after I overdosed, Sara moved me onto the floor and called 911. Her house happened to be close to a hospital and fire station, and that may be the only reason I survived. My heart stopped and I died for a few minutes. Sara dumped all the evidence before the paramedics arrived. I was unconscious with no pulse. I hadn't breathed in four minutes. They used a defibrillator to restart my heart and injected me with Narcan to revive me. I had a huge surge of adrenaline when I came to. I tried to get up but was being restrained.

I heard voices asking, "Are you there? Can you hear us?"

I looked down to see that my shirt had been cut off and medical equipment was hanging all over me. All I could think about was my designer jeans. "Don't cut off my jeans! These are my favorite jeans." My jeans were important to me. They were all that I had.

The paramedics carried me out into the March cold on a gurney. I was angry they'd taken off all of my clothes. I was nothing but skin and bones and I was shivering violently. By the time I arrived at the hospital, my anger changed to sadness. I was crying like a baby because I didn't understand what was happening to me. In treatment, I didn't think I had a serious problem, so I judged everyone else. *Look at all you crackheads. What's wrong with you?* But just three short weeks later I was overdosing on heroin. Normal people might be able to rationalize taking a few painkillers here and there. Normal people cannot rationalize shooting up with heroin. I had entered a whole new realm of danger that was not socially acceptable. Heroin felt seedy and dirty to me. I sobbed when I realized how far down I had fallen. My feelings made me sick to my stomach and I just wanted to get high again so I could make them go away. That's what drug addiction looks like.

At the hospital, the police questioned me. I refused to tell them anything about Sara. A nurse asked me who I wanted to call and I didn't know. I couldn't remember Mom's or Dad's number, so I gave Amber's number. Amber called Dad and they arrived at the hospital together. They knew I'd just gotten out of treatment and they were confused. "We don't understand. You're working and hanging out with your friends again. We thought you solved your problem. We don't know how to help you. It's out of our hands." I wasn't in the mood for that conversation, but I was trapped. *Now Dad wants to talk to me?* Because of the Narcan, I wasn't able to pee. That was required if I wanted to be released from the hospital. I listened to Dad and Amber drill me for two hours. I couldn't take anymore, so I willingly accepted a catheter so I could get out of there. I was desperate to get high again.

After I was finally released, Dad continued to lecture me on the way out the door. "We don't know what to do with you. We thought you were sober. Treatment obviously didn't work. You need to go back." He and Amber didn't understand what I was going through. How could they? I didn't even understand. Sobriety was a brand new endeavor for me and I didn't know how to do it. My first experience in treatment was the first time I learned there was an option besides using. For a lot of people, it takes multiple stints in treatment centers to be convinced that the alternate option is worth trying. I wasn't at that point yet.

Dad and Amber left in disgust because they weren't willing to stand around and watch me die. My car was parked close by at Sara's apartment. I drove home alone and in utter despair. I was shocked and didn't know how to proceed. *I just died for a few minutes. What am I supposed to do now?* I had no support system, no one to talk to. I felt similar to the way I felt after slitting my wrist, but with more shame. Again, I wasn't relieved to be alive.

I was ashamed because my family expected me to be healed. I had that expectation too, but it's not that easy. It's incredibly difficult because the disease of addiction had convinced me I didn't actually have a disease. *Maybe I'm not really an addict. I can use again and things will work out differently this time.* My family discovered the magnitude of my problem and that was embarrassing. I disappointed Dad, myself, and the whole family. *I'm supposed to be better than this. What the fuck is going on? How do I stop it?*

I walked into my apartment to find my roommates sleeping. I laid down in my bed with thoughts racing through my head. I stared at the ceiling for hours because I couldn't fall asleep. *What the hell just happened today?* I couldn't return to normal after experiencing such trauma. My line in the sand had moved too far. I was disgusted with myself. I could feel a minor panic attack coming on as I thought about the day's events. Intense feelings were surfacing. *I gotta run from this. It's too much for me to handle.*

I waited until the sun came up and then did what any good drug addict would do—I looked for a way to get high again. It sounds crazy after almost dying the day before, but addiction is an allergy of the body and an obsession of the mind. Those first two hits of heroin set off a craving that I couldn't stop. *I want more.* I called Sara, but she didn't answer. I called a few other people and finally got ahold of Jim, another person I met in the treatment center. We made plans to meet and get high. I needed to run from my guilt, shame, and remorse. I couldn't handle the fact that I had just died or the feelings of dirtiness and inadequacy that came along with it. I was feeling a thousand emotions and they were surfacing in confusing ways. My using really took off from there in order to bury my emotions and sense of worthlessness.

I got high that day, the next day, and the day after that. I spent the next thirty days doing nothing but getting high. I didn't care what drugs were available. I wouldn't even ask what they were before doing them. I just asked for more. I liked all of them. In the beginning, the mood altering effects of painkillers made me the happiest. When that stopped working for me, I had to move on to stronger substances. Cocaine excited me because there was an undercurrent of illicitness that came with it. It was usually hidden from everyone else, so I felt like I was in on a secret when I did cocaine. Heroin was similar, but with more danger. It felt exceptionally dark and worse than all the other drugs I had done. Cocaine can be a party drug, but heroin is not a party drug. It's done in the dark underbelly of society. That's where I ended up. And shooting heroin involved walking a very thin line between life and death. That thrilled me. I wanted to die.

Getting high numbed my emotional pain enough to make it tolerable. I was an empty shell of a human and didn't possess the will to live anymore. I was in survival mode at all times. I only got high, ate a little, and slept. All other bodily functions ceased to work. I shot up so much that my arms were completely torn up and always covered in blood. They looked like two thick red plastic baseball bats that kids play with. If my family had seen me, they would have been horrified. But they never saw me. I resided in an isolated cave of addiction with drugs as my only companions.

Fuck! I've got to get out of here. The pain. My stomach. I can't eat. I grip the metal frame of my bed as another wave of nausea crashes into me. It's why they call it riding the cot. I feel like I have the worst flu of my entire life. I'm on day three of the five-day medical detox at Parkside and all I can do is sit on this bed and think. How did I get here? I can't make it two more days. It's not worth it. All I want is to get high. I know it will take away all of the sickness.

This is why it's almost impossible to detox on your own. Day three is the worst and then at some point during day four or five, you finally make it to the other side. I've never made it to the other side on my own. Believe me, I've tried many times. The days are filled with shaking, twitching, and sweating. Usually around the midpoint of day three, the chills, pain, and vomiting become unbearable and I can't take the agony anymore. Then I'm right back out there, calling the same people and getting high again. It's a never-ending cycle.

Here I'm taking other drugs that make the withdrawal from heroin a little gentler. It's still so painful and miserable. Diarrhea sends me to the bathroom yet again. Even though I try to avoid it, I catch sight of my reflection in the mirror—ghostly white, covered in sweat. I can't do it. I have to get out of here.

Walking back to my bed is unbearable. Excruciating aches have settled deep inside every single one of my bones. I must be twenty pounds lighter, but I feel like I've been encased in concrete.

I'm sure an hour has passed when I make it back to my bed. I wish an hour had passed. Then I would be closer. I glance at the clock to see it's been only five minutes. I feel that the inside of my pants are drenched with sweat when I sit back down. I stare at the wall.

I have to get out of here. I have to get high. More pain. I grip the bed. I stare at the wall.

CHAPTER 8

ROUND TWO

After a month of nonstop heroin use, I went back into treatment because Dad told me I could return to work if I got my shit together. Although I deserved to be fired, Dad wanted to help and believed I was better off working than not working. I should have been dead and he knew it.

I still had insurance and was able to use it to pay for my stay at Parkside Treatment Center. Detox was much more difficult the second time. When I entered Talbot Hall for the first time, I'd only been drinking and taking painkillers. I was a full-fledged heroin addict by the time I made it to Parkside. Medical detox was excruciating. I was forced back into the regimented days of treatment and expected to interact with others again. They expected me to be nice to people while I felt like I had the worst sickness of my life. *I can't do it*. I was so raw. Everything hurt, inside and out.

Inpatient treatment lasted ten days and, about midway through, I started to see exactly how much my thirty days of using had damaged my life. *What the hell have I done?* I had no friends left. I'd been sharing an apartment with two other guys, but I never interacted with them. They were living responsible lives while I was always alone in my room doing drugs. I never emerged from my cave to talk to them. My old friends knew I was an addict and wanted nothing to do with me. I acted crazy and out of control around them. Hanging out with me was too much to bear; my sadness was overwhelming for everyone. My family also distanced themselves from me. They understood that I had become a tornado, ripping people's lives apart. I still wasn't over the trauma of my parents' divorce because I never talked about my feelings with anyone. I initially began using to run away from the pain, but suddenly, I had become the person causing deep pain for the people who loved me. I was the problem in everyone's lives.

As all of that hit me, I started to listen to the things they were telling me at Parkside. I actually listened. For the first time, I was willing to find out what I needed to do to stay sober. I learned that it would require loss and grieving. I had to let go of the very things, drugs and alcohol, that enabled me to cope with life. Losing them felt like someone important to me had died. It left an enormous hole in me that I didn't know how to fill. It felt like I was giving up my identity. Even though I didn't want to be the same person anymore, letting go of that identity still involved grief. I finally wanted a sober life, but I couldn't conceptualize it yet. *What will it look like?* The thought of it was terrifying.

I was finally willing to listen because I knew I was in trouble. I'd lost everyone in my life and I was about to lose my job. My pain was great enough to convince me that I had a problem. Things had escalated quickly and I kept moving my line in the sand that separated what I was willing to do from what I was not willing to do. Every time I moved that line, I sold a little piece of my soul in exchange for drugs. I was willing to do almost anything in order to get high. *If I lost my job, would I rob people to support my habit? Will I have to physically hurt people to rob them?* My disease would have been happy to tell me those behaviors were acceptable. At Parkside, that became clear to me and I knew I wasn't that kind of person. *Whoa, that is scary. I don't rob people. I'm not violent.*

I needed to rediscover the true Taylor. That required help. In treatment, they told me I needed to go to meetings, work the steps, and get a sponsor. I said, "okay" to all of it. I was ready to surrender. *What do I need to do?*

I already had a sponsor because I had to get one before leaving Talbot Hall. They explained to me that a sponsor is someone who can be a spiritual guide through the twelve steps and a sounding board for ideas. I was supposed to consult my sponsor before making any big decisions because in early sobriety, it is very difficult to distinguish right from wrong. I was always wrong. We addicts continually lie to ourselves. The voice we are most likely to hear is our disease rather than our true self. I didn't really understand the importance of a sponsor when I was in Talbot Hall. I simply viewed the requirement as a hoop through which I was required to jump if I wanted to be released.

I didn't know who to choose as my sponsor. I was told to pick someone who had what I wanted, but I hadn't met the right person yet. Instead, I selected someone I hadn't even met. I called a hotline for alcoholism and talked the person who answered into becoming my sponsor.

"I'm at Talbot Hall and I need a sponsor to get out of here. Will you be my sponsor?"

"Well, that's not really how it works."

"I know, but I don't have anyone else to ask. Please be my sponsor."

John eventually agreed to become my first sponsor. He didn't actually have what I wanted, but I didn't know that at the time. It wasn't his fault. I randomly picked him instead of choosing a sponsor the correct way. John was an alcoholic and didn't understand my multiple addictions. Even though all addictions are similar, an alcoholic can usually remain a functioning member of society for much longer. Alcohol is legal and does not have to be completely hidden from the world, and it usually kills a person more slowly. The heroin addict operates underground and flirts with death every single day. John hadn't experienced that side of addiction. Because I didn't feel like he understood me, I wasn't willing to share everything with him. And I needed to share all of my secrets with a sponsor in order to get better.

Although I was trying harder at Parkside, the fact that I kept John as my sponsor demonstrated that I wasn't entirely prepared to get sober. My attitude toward the other suggestions for recovery was similar. I was picking and choosing, buffet style, what I was willing to do. *I'll do this stuff, but I'm not doing any of that shit over there.* I was given material to read but only read the things I felt like reading. I was told there were twelve steps to recovery, but I only did the ones I wanted to do. For example, the fifth step required me to share a moral inventory—all the good and bad shit that I'd done—with my sponsor. I didn't want to share that information with anyone, not even John. I believed I had surrendered, but my surrender was not one hundred percent. I simply wasn't there yet.

I did keep trying. After ten days of inpatient treatment, I spent a month in intensive outpatient treatment (IOP). It was held in a classroom setting and was meant to give me the skills to reintegrate into society. It was scary to walk out the door of Parkside, and IOP helped me apply the techniques I'd learned in treatment to my life. I spent eight hours each day talking about addiction and recovery. Sometimes the sessions were connected to twelve-step meetings in order to ensure we were comfortable with attending those on our own. Most of the people in IOP were more willing to do the work of recovery than the people I met during inpatient treatment. I got to know some great people in IOP who are still my friends today.

After IOP, I went back to work and slowly started putting the pieces of my life back together. I saw the fog beginning to lift from my psyche, and my outlook became more positive. I still didn't believe I had the playbook to life, but I was searching for it. One big obstacle to sobriety remained though—my huge ego. In order to fully commit to sobriety, I needed to have my ego shattered. I had to become humble, teachable, and willing to learn about everything that was required for a sober life. Instead, I resisted adopting every suggestion for recovery. I went to some meetings, but I didn't go to enough meetings. I only had one foot in the program.

Still, my life was improving. During my month of using, I didn't work and I spent all my money on drugs. I lost everything. In my newfound sobriety, I was selling a lot at work and had plenty of money coming in. I got an apartment of my own. I bought a fancy car and put rims on it. Things were going really well for me, at least externally. I had financial success, but on the inside, I still didn't feel whole. Something was missing. I put too much stock in material gain and didn't do enough work on the tough task of personal development. I didn't spend the time at meetings or gaining depth and understanding of the recovery process.

One of the best gifts of my sobriety was meeting my good friend Kris. He was seven years sober when I met him at a meeting and he was willing to help guide me in recovery. Kris is the type of person who goes out of his way to do anything he can for others who are struggling with addiction. He's a fucking saint. I have no doubt about that. It may be because he struggled so much. Kris is a recovering crackhead and the chance of a crack addict staying sober is even smaller than the slim chance that a heroin addict will stay sober. Because the compulsion to use crack is typically stronger than with any other drug, crack addicts usually have to work much harder than anyone else to get sober.

Kris introduced himself, gave me his number, and said, "Let's hang out. Let's go to meetings together." I was shocked. *What's wrong with this guy?* No one wanted to hang out with me unless it was to get high. It took a while for me to be convinced that Kris really was interested in getting to know me. He was the first person who genuinely wanted to help. His approach to sobriety was infectious. Kris and I went to meetings together and I touched base with him every couple of days. It felt incredibly good to finally have a person in my life who understood exactly what I was going through. As our bond strengthened, I started making some other sober friends and felt like I was part of a community for the first time. I began loosening the grip on my loner mentality and realized I had to have allies in recovery if I was going to stay sober. For once, I understood that I couldn't do it alone.

Kris and I are on a winding motorcycle ride through Hocking Hills on this oppressively hot summer day. The foliage canopy over the back roads provides shade and relief. Riding clears my head and helps me focus. Spending time with Kris gives me stability and hope. Being surrounded by trees reminds me how far I've come and makes me believe I can continue on my journey out of the dark forest of addiction.

I'm a good rider, but Kris is better, so I follow his lead. We're going forty miles per hour when we take the curve. I hit some loose gravel and the next thing I know my bike slips out from under me and into the woods. I land violently on the hard pavement. Instant total body pain.

Kris sees that I'm pale as a ghost when he arrives at my side. My collarbone, shoulder, and ankles are throbbing. My jeans are mostly ripped off and I'm covered in road rash. Thank God I'm wearing a helmet, but I think it may have crushed my collarbone. I can't raise my left arm.

Kris calls an ambulance. I moan and writhe in pain while we wait. The smallest movements are agony. There's no way I can lift myself off the ground. Kris warns me not to try.

When EMS arrives, the first words out of my mouth are, "I'm in recovery and only eight months sober. I can't have any narcotic painkillers. I just have to deal with the pain."

"Are you sure?"

"I'm sure."

They strap me to a gurney and load me into the ambulance. Each time we turn or hit a bump, the pain is so excruciating that I almost pass out. I hope to pass out. I pray to pass out. It doesn't happen.

This is more pain than I have ever felt. How will I do this without drugs? I have to do this without drugs. God, please give me the strength. I can't go back. I can't go back.

CHAPTER 9

AN OLD FRIEND

Kris was my brother in sobriety and had such a positive influence on me that I wanted to spend as much time with him as possible. We enjoyed long scenic rides together. It was a significant departure from the reckless motorcycle days of my past. I wanted to strengthen my grasp on sobriety, but my disease had another agenda. It showed me exactly how powerful it was. I was vulnerable to using again because I wasn't doing all the work necessary to remain sober. I viewed the suggestions as optional instead of mandatory for my sobriety. By not working carefully through the steps, I was limiting my potential for recovery. I was just waiting for an excuse to get high again, and medical necessity was the perfect excuse.

Kris accompanied me to the hospital and stayed with me while I was treated. X-rays showed that my collarbone was broken and my shoulder was separated. The doctor asked me if I wanted any pain medication. I said no. I was stone cold sober when they put me into a figure eight brace that pulled my shoulder blades together to reset the collar bone. The pain was severe and my resolve began to waiver. The doctor told me the pain was going to linger because the collarbone is surrounded by so many nerves. He suggested I might need to take some painkillers. I looked at Kris for direction and he said, "Call your sponsor."

I used Kris's phone to call John. He didn't know what to say. John never had a drug problem and wasn't qualified to guide me in the situation. John advised me to take the painkillers if I needed them. "You should probably listen to the doctor. It sounds like you're in a lot of pain." When I heard those words, my disease immediately started to take over. *Sure, you can take them. It's no big deal.*

I looked at the doctor and said, "I'm an addict. Don't give me the strong stuff. Just give me enough to relieve some of the pain." John and my doctor both told me it was alright. I saw a green light. *What could possibly go wrong?*

My addiction was sitting dormant and waiting to pounce. As soon as I took the morphine, I immediately knew it was game over. The pain in my shoulder didn't disappear. Instead, I felt a wave of euphoria. The morphine high was an old friend who I missed. It felt so good. I laid in the hospital bed without a care in the world for the first time in eight months. It took about thirty minutes for me to convince myself that I wasn't really an addict. It was that easy. *What I did wasn't so bad. I never really lost my job. I never had an accident while drinking and driving. I didn't hurt anyone. What was the problem?* I quickly talked myself out of the program of recovery and back into using.

The doctor sent me home with a prescription for Percocet, which I filled immediately. At home, I looked at the instructions on the bottle and decided I couldn't take it as prescribed. *These never messed me up. The doctor has to understand that I can't take only what is prescribed for most people. They don't work on me like they work on others. I'm in too much pain.* My mind created a story about why I needed to take more, and within fourteen hours, I took thirty pills. The next morning, I looked into the pill bottle and freaked out when I saw there were only five pills left. *I need more. I have insurance. I can call another doctor.*

Thus began several weeks of doctor shopping. I convinced four other doctors to write me prescriptions for painkillers. The fifth doctor looked up my filled prescriptions and told me I couldn't have any more. "Too much time has passed since you broke your collarbone. You don't need the strong painkillers anymore," he told me. *I do need them. I have to have them.*

I contacted the same guy at work who sold me the first pills when I switched from alcohol to painkillers. Bob agreed to sell me some more pills. When I met him, I had a fleeting moment of clarity. *A month ago I was sober. In the blink of an eye, I'm in the ghetto buying Percocet. How did I get here again?* It was the first time I understood why recovering addicts describe the disease of addiction as cunning, baffling, and powerful. I realized it was cunning because it came at me through an injury. It was baffling because I couldn't figure out how I got back to using so quickly after the hard work of staying sober for eight months. It was powerful because I couldn't extract myself from its grip, even when I became aware of it. I wanted to stop, but it was too difficult. The bondage was too strong. *Don't worry. You're not using as much as you were before.* I was lying to myself. My disease convinced me I wasn't really an addict.

Soon, Percocet lost its effectiveness and I had to graduate to stronger painkillers once again. From there, it was a steep and easy slide back to heroin. *Before I went to that goddamn treatment center, I was taking Oxycontin and shooting heroin. I guess I could do that again because it's cheaper.* Yes, it's cheaper, but it also kills a person faster. I didn't consider any of the consequences. My disease morphed again and convinced me that shooting heroin again would be alright as long as I did less than before. That's the type of lie we addicts tell ourselves. The denial is thick. Suddenly, I was sticking needles in my arms all the time, I was bankrupt, and I felt worse than ever. *My life is totally fucked up. My arms are about to fall off. How did I let this happen again? Didn't I have a good amount of sobriety? I'm lying to myself again.* My whirlwind of denial became a freight train of destruction that was unstoppable. Addiction didn't take that much from me before, but it was about to take everything. My eight months of sobriety and prosperity were wiped away in a matter of weeks because they were built on sand.

The emptiness that initially drove me to alcohol and drugs was still inside. I bought material things instead of finding value within myself. I experienced momentary euphoria when I purchased things such as motorcycles, fancy cars, and nice houses. I searched outside of myself for validation. Many nonaddicts do that as well, but given my predisposition for addiction, it was too dangerous for me. It was easy for me to use material goods to fill the same void that I previously filled with drugs and alcohol. I wasn't paying enough attention to my actions. The void inside was not filled with meaningful things. It was merely hidden from view and was waiting to swallow me back into the darkness.

———

We're waiting in the gas station parking lot. The place changes each day, but the routine never does. It's the same never-ending cycle of insanity. I'm in the driver's seat and Nurse Donna is next to me. She's not even a goddamn nurse. She's just someone who can get me any drug I want. Her clothes smell like rusted water pipes and cigarettes. I don't like her, but I need her. She has the connection. I don't want the connection. I never want it. I don't want to go to jail. This shit is serious. Mexican cartels.

Nurse Donna needs me because I have money. She will make the purchase. She will put it in her pocket. She will take the rap if it comes to that. In exchange, she will get high too.

Both of us are glistening with sweat, shaking and twitching. Withdrawal feels like the flu. The conversation we're trying to have over the blaring music makes no sense. I'm sure of it. I'm also sure I will die if he doesn't get here soon. I need it. This has to happen right now. It's lifesaving medication. An inhaler for the asthmatic. That's how desperate I am. How desperate we both are.

He drives by in the gray Chevy Malibu. Nurse Donna immediately opens the door and throws up. It's user anticipation. We are animals who are about to be fed. We know the high is so close now and we're excited.

He always makes us wait. My heart is racing. We've been here for forty minutes today. I pull the car out of the parking lot and follow him down one of the neighborhood streets. He stops. I stop. Nurse Donna quickly hops into his car and buys the heroin. When she opens the passenger door to get back into my car, I open my door and throw up too. She doesn't even blink an eye. It's normal for us, but if a nonaddict saw this, he would ask, "What the hell is happening?"

I don't usually throw up though. It gives me a brief moment of clarity. What the fuck am I doing? Am I an animal? I've crossed another line. Yes, I've gotten this bad. I throw up because I'm getting ready to use. I need it that bad. It's fucking crazy! This is the dark side of addiction that people don't understand. The lowest place to be. Rock bottom. For a moment, I know this is not who I am. But how will I ever not do this? I don't know how to live without drugs and alcohol. It has a huge hold on me and it will be impossible for me to get out of it. Unless I kill myself. That's the only exit in sight. Taking even the slightest honest look at myself makes me realize I would rather die than acknowledge and deal with all of my problems.

He drives away. We have to satisfy our thirst. There's no way we can make it home first, so I drive to a nearby *carwash and pull into one of the five stalls. Nurse Donna and I get high together in the car. We can't live without this. We're beyond repair.*

CHAPTER 10

BEYOND REPAIR

My relapse into heroin addiction coincided with my first marriage. I met Tiffany shortly before my motorcycle accident. We were introduced by a mutual friend and I felt an immediate attraction to her. During our first conversation, I found out her brother was also in recovery. Our relationship became serious after my accident because Tiffany moved in and took on the role of caregiver for me as I healed from my injuries. A few months later, we got married. I was high on our wedding day.

Tiffany and I were both unstable, and our speedy union was disastrous. She was stone cold sober, but was struggling with an eating disorder. Even though Tiffany didn't share my addiction, she had a similar level of self-hate. We both had low self-esteem and felt empty inside. Similar to my drug use, her unhealthy relationship with food was born from the desire to fill the void. I was attracted to her because she was a reflection of me. On top of her eating disorder, she felt the pain of having an addict in the family. She wanted to save me.

Our marriage was marked by codependency and turmoil. Tiffany was beautiful, feisty, and forward. Like me, she was a fighter. We shared a gritty outlook on life. We both felt like we had to fight for everything we got and were willing to do whatever was necessary to get ahead. Tiffany and I both found pleasure in material goods, so we bought fancy cars and an expensive house in an exclusive community. It was all about keeping up with the Joneses. We used our money to mask our struggles, so our life looked great from the outside. In reality, it was incredibly sad and dysfunctional. As usual, the way my life looked from the outside did not match what was really going on inside. I married Tiffany without even really knowing her. I didn't understand that she came with a lot of baggage of her own. All I cared about was getting high. I couldn't see her pain. I had nothing to offer her. *I'm a fucking junkie.*

Tiffany wanted me to get help, but I was not interested. However, I did have brief moments when I remembered the good times of my sobriety and wanted to return to them. Those eight months were the only time in my life when I felt like I was getting closer to living the life I was meant to live. It was devastating to get a glimpse of the good life and then resume a life of addiction. *Everything was so good. How do I get back to that?* My already low level of self-respect reached new depths as I stuck myself with needles every day. I was using more than ever.

Tiffany and I still lived in our expensive house even though we were not paying for it. We never made more than a couple of mortgage payments. I was broke, but we tried to keep up the façade of having money. After Tiffany left for work each day, I went out to buy heroin and get high. I always returned home before she did so we could have dinner together. Then I would shoot up one more time while she took a bath. The routine was comforting in the midst of our crumbling life.

I had managed to keep my job at Dad's company and made a lot of money when I was sober. But soon after I broke my collarbone, it became clear to Dad that I was using again. I was slurring my words, acting irresponsibly, and not showing up for work. Dad knew I needed to go back into treatment and couldn't continue working. He didn't fire me in person though. He called me while I was on my honeymoon with Tiffany in Cancun. My response was, "Whatever. I'll figure it out when I get home." I hung up the phone without emotion. I thought my firing was the company's loss instead of mine. I still believed I was indispensable. *Even with my problems, I'm still better than all the other sales guys combined. They can't do it without me.* Dad reached the conclusion that they didn't need me anymore because I was too much of a liability. I only became angry about being fired when I found out the company wasn't going to pay me some of the commission money I had earned. I knew I was unemployable and wasn't going to earn anything else. *Fuck you guys.* I needed to find a new source of money to support my addiction.

I was hired to do sales for a Cadillac dealership. They only hired me because I was already driving a Cadillac that I bought there. They thought I was part of the family even though I was literally unemployable. I was working hard to keep up appearances though. Tiffany bought me nice clothes, so I looked good on the outside. But inside, I was dying from my disease. I snorted drugs off my desk at work and off of a CD case in the bathroom. I actually thought I had stepped back from my addiction a bit when I started my new job because I returned to snorting heroin instead of shooting it. I believed I was successfully managing my addiction since I wasn't getting as high anymore. I was lying to myself.

Even though I was working, I struggled to buy enough heroin to satisfy my cravings because I had to start helping Tiffany with some of our expenses again. I gave her most of the money I made. One day, I received a twelve hundred dollar draw at work and gave Tiffany all but two hundred of it. I needed to score some drugs with the money I kept. I called my friend Jim—one of the addicts I met during my first stint at Talbot Hall. He was a crack addict who had been in and out of treatment centers for fourteen years. He could never put together any time in sobriety. Jim talked like a hippy and dressed like a thug. He was a criminal who was constantly trying to take advantage of people. He talked too much and was full of shit. He was a skeevy character and no one trusted him. Jim and I went to some meetings together after we got out of treatment. That led to us getting high together since neither of us was serious about getting sober. Jim became my go-to guy whenever I was in a pinch. I used him as a middle man because of his numerous connections.

Jim drove up to the dealership with two other people in the car, a driver and a guy named Dollar. Dollar and I never got along because he was always ripping people off or robbing them. He was a stick-up boy. I knew he was not to be trusted, ever. I handed Jim my money and said, "You've got to bring me some drugs because I'm stuck here at work." Even though I didn't trust Dollar, I really considered Jim a friend. They left with my money and didn't return. After two hours I got angry and started calling Jim obsessively. By the time I got off work, I had called him fifteen times and was completely bent out of shape. *Those fuckers just stole my only money to get high with.* I was feeling sick from withdrawal.

I knew where Jim lived and I was determined to get my money back. I went home, grabbed my AR-15 and got back in the car, still wearing my black work trench coat. I drove over to Jim's apartment building with a semi-automatic military grade assault rifle in the back of my Cadillac. It was an uncharacteristically warm fall day, so many of his neighbors were sitting outside on their patios. When they saw me get out of the car with my gun, they all went inside. I climbed the stairs to Jim's apartment and looked in the window. I saw his girlfriend and a little boy in the living room. Jim wasn't home. *You can't hurt them.* Still angry, I walked back downstairs, took a bullet out of my gun, and put it in an envelope. I wrote a note that said, "Today was your lucky day. I was here to collect my money. Real friends don't do this to each other." I put the envelope on Jim's doormat and left.

Of course Jim was pissed when he found the bullet on his porch. He called me that night and we had a yelling match, which neither of us won. Jim and I didn't have a real friendship since we were both addicts. No authentic bond can be formed when you're simply getting high with someone. Still, I thought he was my friend and he stole from me. I wanted him to pay. I feel like God stepped in and made sure Jim wasn't home when I arrived so I wouldn't cross another line. I don't think I would have shot him because I didn't want to hurt anyone. I did want to scare the living shit out of him though. I was like an animal whose only instinct is to survive. I needed those drugs to live. In the note, I told Jim, "Today was your lucky day." In reality, it was my lucky day.

As I drove home, I thought to myself, *what the hell?* My whole life was crumbling around me. All of Tiffany's income was going toward paying our other bills, so I was out of cash. I only had one credit card left that wasn't maxed out. At the time, it was popular for people to install little TVs in their cars. I saw a way to use that fad to fund my heroin habit. I went to the electronics store and bought several car TVs and then gave them to my dealer in exchange for drugs. I repeated the transaction until I reached my credit card limit. Tiffany flipped out each time the credit card bill arrived in the mail. My addiction was continually burying us further in debt, but I didn't care. I only cared about finding a way to buy more drugs. *How do I supply my habit?*

My answer was to start trading guns to drug dealers. Throughout my life, I collected guns as a hobby. I used them for target practice. I had only recently begun building an arsenal. Using was causing me to become more and more paranoid. I was strung out and I didn't trust anyone. I needed to protect myself and to defend my addiction and my behavior. I was never a violent person, but guns made me feel tough.

Guns were the only things I owned that had value. I was so desperate to get high that I was willing to give them up. And I was willing to trade them to known felons who weren't even allowed to own guns. I was dealing with a guy named Petey and his partner, Face. Sometimes I called Face and he sent Petey to meet me, or I called Petey and he sent

Face. They kept me guessing so I never knew who I was going to get. Petey and Face were both part of a major drug trafficking ring, but Face was the only one who really scared me. *That is such a creepy nickname. How did he get it?*

I had twelve guns in my collection, so I started trading the cheaper guns first. I typically got seventy-five percent of the gun's value in heroin. Then I would go home with a hundred bags and stash them all around the house. I stashed needles everywhere too. I usually couldn't find all of them when I looked later because I was so high that I didn't remember where I put them. Eventually, I had to start trading my more expensive guns to keep up with my habit.

One day, I set up a meeting with Face and decided to trade my AR-15, the same gun I took to Jim's house. It was an expensive gun. I pulled up to the curb to wait for Face and looked at the rifle in the back seat. It was a deadly weapon, and the last place it should have been was in the hands of a drug dealing gang member. I didn't believe that was any concern of mine though. I just wanted to get high. When Face pulled up in his green Plymouth van, the thought crept into my mind that I didn't have to give him the gun. I contemplated using it to rob him instead. *My rifle will overpower any gun he could possibly have in there. All I have to do is pull it on him and he will shit his pants and hand over anything I want. The clip has fifty rounds and I could tear his entire van apart. He probably has a revolver with nine rounds. He can't stop me with that.* I had a huge amount of firepower in my hands and it was tempting me.

Doubts about the ill-conceived plan began to creep into my mind. *Should I do this? Will it start a war? Will they come after my family?*

Then suddenly another voice took over with certainty. *I don't want to hurt anyone. I won't kill someone for drugs. I don't want to go to jail. It's not worth it. Just give him the gun. I don't want it anyway. I just want to get high.* I listened to that voice and looked up to see that Face was becoming agitated about the wait. I slid the gun under my coat and hopped into his car.

"I've got a thousand dollar gun under here."

"What kind?"

"AR-15"

"Oh shit! Hand it to me now!"

Face wanted the gun out of my hands immediately so I handed it to him and said, "I'll trade you for drugs." He passed me thirty pouches of heroin and I was relieved that I wouldn't need to see him again for a few days. I drove myself to work and got high in the bathroom.

I kept moving my line in the sand to make sure I could get more drugs. Putting guns into the hands of drug dealers required me to move it more than I ever expected. *All of the principles I laid out for myself are gone.* The day I traded my AR-15 to Face was a day when I had to make a decision about just how much further I was willing to move that line. My mind was swirling and racing. It was a critical moment because I contemplated physically harming another person. Despite my desperation, I had never done anything like that. I had to make a choice to shoot him or give up the gun. Fortunately, the voice of reason won. *You can't do it, Taylor. Just get the drugs and get out of here.* I chose to trade the gun to pay for drugs instead of doing something that could have sent me to prison. I knew that if I was going to pull a gun on someone, I had to be ready to fire it. Fortunately, I wasn't willing to do that.

We finish getting high in the car wash and then Nurse Donna and I make our way back to the house. We walk the path of wooden boards on top of mud where there should be grass. Piles of trash cover the back yard. The path leads us to the back door of a two story brick house. After we knock, someone looks outside to make sure we're not cops. As soon as he sees Nurse Donna, he removes the boards from the door and lets us in. After we enter, he replaces the boards and barricades us inside.

Being here feels criminal. Guns are everywhere. The kids outside and the bosses on the corner have them. They are also in the dimly lit house. Only one light works in the entire place. And there is no natural light because all of the windows are either boarded up or covered with sheets and blinds so no one can see in. The front door is never opened and no one is allowed to enter through it. This is the ghetto.

We walk down the hall, past the sleeping crackheads. They never wake up until late afternoon, while we heroin addicts are up bright and early to get high. Nurse Donna tried to clean up a bit, but the house is always dirty and covered in cobwebs. The once white walls, plastic blinds, and ripped linoleum floors are all yellowed from smoke. The whole place reeks of cigarettes and dirty feet. All of the furniture is from the seventies and the couches are marked with burn holes. Everything is decaying, including the people.

I make my way to the kitchen table and sit down on one of the four old, disgusting chairs. The pot in the center of the table overflows with cigarettes and ashes. The fridge is even older than the furniture and has to be latched shut like a cooler. Crack was cooked last night on the stove next to the old food that attracts cockroaches. No one ever eats any real food because we are only here to get high. The bathroom is disgusting and I don't even know if there is running water in the house. It doesn't matter because we don't need it. The house is uninhabitable, but I will stay here all day.

CHAPTER 11

HOPELESS

I graduated from snorting back to shooting heroin as my addiction intensified, and I suddenly felt immersed in the dark underbelly of society. I met a woman known as Nurse Donna, who lived in a crack house with her husband Trace in a very seedy part of the city. I began hanging out there because the heroin was plentiful. I was the pretty boy who drove a nice car to a house in the hood. There was a massive amount of drug activity in the neighborhood and people sold drugs right on the street in broad daylight. Hoppers ran around and delivered drugs to the cars passing through. The hoppers were teenagers because kids can't be sent to prison for selling drugs. They had rotating shifts, so they came inside the house to eat during their breaks. The whole operation ran like a business. The hoppers delivered the drugs but didn't take the money. Trace's nephew was the business man who handled all of the money. He was in charge of the drug ring. Nurse Donna and Trace were addicts themselves and were used as pawns to attract other addicts. I was one of those addicts.

As I got high in the house every day, I could hear gun shots related to the drug activity outside.

Jim introduced me to Nurse Donna. She controlled the block and was the queen of the neighborhood. Nurse Donna had absolutely no money, but she managed her own addiction by capitalizing on her extensive connections to dealers. She had everyone's phone numbers and kept them to herself so we all had to go through her to get what we wanted. She was the gatekeeper. We paid her in drugs and she continually schemed to keep that system functioning to her benefit. It was her business and she was successful at it. She could have been rich had she not been a junkie. Nurse Donna was also a kind of den mother in the house. She protected me and was a twisted version of a mother figure. I didn't like her though. I could only tolerate being in her presence long enough to get the drugs that I needed and get high. That contrasted with some of the other addicts who sought out Nurse Donna and wanted to be in her presence because of her power.

Nurse Donna was wanted on four different counts. She rarely left the house and, when she did, she had to wear a disguise. She only went outside with me because I would drive her where she needed to go. Nurse Donna stayed inside while I started my car. Then she ran out, got in the car, and we drove away immediately. When we arrived at our destination, she had to get inside another house as quickly as possible. Maybe she was just high and paranoid, but there were definitely marshals actively searching for her around the house.

Nurse Donna was a short, heavy woman who was missing teeth. Her once bleached hair had grown out enough that the bottom half of her hair was blonde while the top half was brown. She always smoked cigarettes and had a raspy voice. Nurse Donna earned her name because she had access to every drug imaginable, pharmaceutical or otherwise. She was also very skilled at finding veins. I was never very good with needles, and the more I stuck my arms, the harder it became to find a good spot. I appreciated having professional drug addicts around me. I could always count on their expertise at finding veins so I could get high.

There were usually four or five of us in the house at any time. Nurse Donna was always there. The other people at the crack house covered the spectrum from prostitutes to drug dealers and crackheads. Sometimes we would sit outside on the porch drinking 40s out of brown paper bags. We all looked like stereotypical homeless drug addicts. Our drugs of choice varied between crack, heroin, and pharmaceuticals. Our common bond was that we were there to get high. It was a community, but it was illicit and dirty. I never felt like I fit in because I was considered the rich kid sitting at the table. The others loved me because they thought I had lots of money. Of course, I was only borrowing from credit cards and going more into debt. But I was willing to share some of my stash, so they liked having me there. I didn't like being in the house, but it had what I needed.

I spent every single day in the house because I had to. One day without heroin would make me sick. On a typical day, I left my house at eight in the morning and spent six or more hours there. I returned home at three or four in the afternoon, just before Tiffany got home from work. I spent the entire day getting high and nodding off in my chair. I never slept at the crack house and didn't ever feel like I should be there. I didn't like any of the other people who hung out at the house either. I could still be a chameleon to fit in with them. I needed to stay on their good side because they had access to the drugs that I wanted.

The house was the whole world for Nurse Donna and Trace. Their entire existence revolved around getting drugs for people, helping them get high, getting high themselves, and drinking. They sat around, bull shitted, sold, bought, and did drugs. There was nothing else. No one ever went to work. The house supported the drug habits of everyone on the block. I ended up in the house because Nurse Donna was the only person I knew who had a connection to buy black tar heroin, my drug of choice when I went back to shooting heroin. Snorting China gray was no longer enough because my tolerance was so high. I needed something stronger.

Once I got high each morning, it was easiest to simply stay at the house and continue to get high for the rest of the day. I shot up between ten and fifteen times each day. My arms were covered with track marks and bruises. I had a long black bruise that ran down the length of my left forearm and felt like a piece of coaxial cable. When I was high, I was a goddamn zombie. My body was falling apart and there was nothing going on in my mind. I was extremely zoned out and disconnected. I had no thoughts, no feelings, and no emotions. I had slipped farther down than ever before. It was the worst period of my using. I was literally dying and I didn't care that it was happening. I no longer had flashes of clarity or the sense that I should be living a different way. I was a full-time addict, all day, every day. I was hopeless.

Eventually, I reluctantly returned to Parkside since it was where my period of sobriety began. But it felt different. I didn't want to be there and I didn't want to get sober. Dying sounded like a better option than fighting my way back to sobriety. It was too much work. I was hopeless and didn't have the will to fight. I was so beaten down physically and emotionally that I simply didn't care anymore.

I only lasted two days at Parkside before I left against medical advice. A drug dealer picked me up in the parking lot and I immediately shot up. I continued using heroin every day, and I added cocaine into the mix. I began speedballing, which involves mixing heroin and cocaine and shooting them together. The chances of death from heroin are already high, but mixing it with cocaine makes death much more likely. I wanted to die. I saw no other way out.

I returned to the house and Nurse Donna. She was a strange character in my life. We spent a lot of time together and she looked out for me on some level. I was always the skinny white kid in the room and she never let anyone fuck with me. She was the person I chose to call from Parkside during my third time in treatment. She told me to call a drug dealer named Pete to pick me up. When she heard my voice she said, "I'm so glad you're okay. I know you're struggling with drug addiction and I want to make sure you're alright." For a moment, it felt like she was my mom on the phone. Based on what we were doing together, I don't think it's possible that she actually cared about me. I certainly didn't care about her. I just wanted to keep her and the others wrapped around my finger so I could maintain my connection to the drugs that I wanted.

But maybe Nurse Donna really did like me. She did keep me from dying and I never felt like I was in danger when we were together.

She and the others in the house also knew they were never in any danger with me. To them, I was just a kid who liked to get high all the time. I was only twenty four. The reason I didn't spend even more time in the house was because I was convinced the cops would eventually bust down the door. I needed to protect myself. I knew I didn't belong there.

I finally got out of that house because Tiffany insisted I go back into treatment. She took away my car and access to money. She pinned me into a corner because she was sick of our life together. We fought every single night. The drama was extreme because I was getting high all the time and it was a huge emotional strain on her. I had a routine of shooting up each evening while Tiffany took her bath. Sometimes she caught me in the act, and other times she saw drops of blood soaking through my long-sleeved white shirt. There was no more hiding the extent of my addiction. Tiffany pressured me until I agreed to return to treatment, just a couple of months after my previous stint.

I was scheduled to be admitted to Talbot Hall on Friday, so I went to the house to get high one last time on Thursday. I was upset and freaking out at the idea of going back to the treatment center. Tiffany took my car away from me, so I had to ask Nurse Donna to send someone to pick me up. On the drive over, it felt like I was on my way to hang out with a bunch of dead people. In the house, we had a going away heroin party. Before I left, Nurse Donna said, "I'm really proud of you for taking care of your shit. I've been trying to get sober for thirty years. I've never been able to do it because I like alcohol and drugs too much. I want you to do it all the way." Then she gave me a hug and I never saw her again.

It's my first day back in Talbot Hall. I chose this treatment center because sweets are allowed here. I didn't want to drink only water. The crowd here is really diverse— a bunch of old homeless guys and a few younger people like me. Many have no money, no house, no car, and survive by panhandling. The first time I was in treatment here, I had a good job and didn't really think that I fit in with everyone else. But now I've stepped much closer to them in my heroin addiction. I'm on the verge of being homeless too. I don't want to be here. I don't want to be sober.

All forty of us are sitting around a large table in a conference room at eight o'clock in the morning when Dr. Murphy walks in. We don't look like we belong in a conference room though. A few of us are wearing street clothes, but most of us are in hospital gowns. Underwear and butt cracks are hanging out all over the place. We're all wearing hospital socks with rubber grips on the bottoms.

I remember my first stay in Talbot Hall. I felt defeated by the disease of addiction, and the only way I could deal with that feeling was to be sarcastic and make fun of everyone else. The other young people joined me in that activity.

"I bet he does heroin."

"I bet she does Oxycontin because she looks tore up."

"Wow, it looks like he's lost a lot. I'm not as bad as him. I'll never be that bad. I shouldn't be here."

"It looks like you just drank some wine coolers and fell down the stairs. No big deal. You don't need this. You're free to go home."

"Yep, you need to be here."

"That guy's the biggest junkie in the room."

"Never making it. You're never getting sober."

"That guy's getting sober."

"On the right track."

"She won't make it. She's never getting sober."

We went around the room judging everyone but ourselves. Judging others allowed me to focus on their problems instead of my own. This time around, I still don't want to be here. My attitude is not good, but I am more subdued today. I don't give a fuck anymore.

Dr. Murphy calls roll and lists each person's drug of choice, treatment plan, and stage of recovery. I have to sit here as he goes through every single person. This is his method of team building. He makes sure we all know about each other in an attempt to make it feel like more of a community. The interaction is bizarre and humiliating. Dr. Murphy also reads off a list of everyone's prescriptions.

"Mr. Hunt. Buspar. What do you have this for?"

He knows what it's for, but I have to answer, "It's for anxiety, sir."

"All right. Do you have anxiety?"

"Yes, I do."

"How do I know it's not just from coming off of the drugs?"

"I don't know. You guys prescribed it for me."

"Okay, you've been here thirteen hours. We'll see how you're doing tomorrow. It's going to be a rough few days."

CHAPTER 12

ROCK BOTTOM

It was difficult to get me into treatment the final time. Tiffany wanted to help me get sober, but I wasn't willing. As a couple, we had a good time for a while, but we weren't having fun anymore. It felt terrible for both of us. I was using so much that I couldn't even pretend to keep it together. I nodded off by seven o'clock each evening. Tiffany wanted to spend time with me and she wanted intimacy, but I couldn't even stay awake for her. My body stopped functioning. My problems in the bedroom, my inability to even use the bathroom, and the pains associated with that convinced her that I was in serious trouble. If that wasn't enough, the house was covered in evidence of my drug use. I shot up in the bathroom every day, and there was still blood on the floor when she took her bath later. My addiction was devastating for Tiffany and for my health. She had to check my pulse every day just to make sure I was still alive. She lived that nightmare over and over and put increased pressure on me to get sober each day.

My body continued to decline and I could never seem to get warm. I had no fat left on my emaciated body. At six feet, three inches tall, I weighed only 148 pounds. I was so cold that I felt like my insides were shaking. It was painful, and I could only warm up by taking hot baths. I rarely consumed anything besides sugar. I ate candy, drank soda, and occasionally ate some fast food. I couldn't eat because food wouldn't move through my system. I had horrible problems with digestion. I hit rock bottom. No previous period compared to the danger I was constantly in from using, the people with whom I was hanging out, the places I went, the amount of damage I was doing to my body, and the awful way I looked. I felt gross, so I can only imagine what other people must have felt around me. I'm sure my decline was sad to watch. It was a slow suicide and I was dying right in front of Tiffany.

My addiction was painful for her, so she became more proactive about trying to change things. She took ownership of my problem and determined to get me sober. While I was out getting high, Tiffany was searching for me. She walked up and down dangerous streets trying to find me. The people I was with helped me hide from her. She was a petite blonde woman banging on the doors of drug dealers and entering houses neither one of us had any business being in. Tiffany was determined to save me from those people, but I only needed to be saved from myself. Instead of believing it was my responsibility to get sober, she asked the dealers, "Why are you selling drugs to him when you know he's struggling with addiction?" But she had things backward because I searched the dealers out in order to buy drugs. They sold to me because they were drug dealers. They were not the problem. I was the problem.

Tiffany knew me during my brief sobriety and she wanted to get back to that. But trying to help me prevented her from working on her own struggles. She was so focused on trying to save me that she let herself deteriorate. Tiffany was in pain and she turned up the pressure on me to get help. She did everything she could to make it more difficult for me to continue using. We had terrible fights all the time because I wanted to keep getting high and that was unacceptable to her. She finally told me that I could either go back to the treatment center or live on the streets by myself.

Inpatient treatment was expensive. I no longer had health insurance and we didn't have the money to pay for it ourselves. Tiffany worked out a payment plan for half of the cost and got a church to donate the other half to us so we didn't have a huge bill at the end. It didn't really matter because we were broke and were going to lose the house and cars anyway. Tiffany still fought hard to keep things together as much as possible. It was difficult because no one in my family wanted anything to do with us. Most of my family members didn't even attend our wedding. They weren't willing to watch me self-destruct.

Tiffany was living with the wreckage of everything I did to ruin us financially. I realized that if I got sober, I would have to deal with that wreckage too. I didn't want to do it. I thought the better option was death. *Everyone would be better off without me.* I became depressed as I contemplated whether life was worth fighting for. I broke down and cried many times, but didn't understand why I was crying. The truth was that everything about my life was sad. I was a shell of a person and didn't even know myself anymore. I had no personality left, only animal instincts. I didn't understand how Tiffany could possibly love me. I may have blamed her for some of my problems, but I was lucky to have her. I would not have gotten sober if she hadn't pushed me to do it.

During my ten days in Talbot Hall, I didn't sleep a wink. I didn't want to do the work required to get sober again. The task seemed monumental. I was beaten down so low that my soul was only a faint flicker of a flame. The veil between life and death was paper thin. I had a long distance to travel from not caring to wanting to live again. I didn't think I could do it.

Only after four days of medical detox did I realize that I had been given another chance to regain my dignity and put my life back together. I knew it was time to face all of the things from which I'd been running for so long—my parents' divorce, my self-hate, and my fear that I didn't have the playbook to life. The fifth day was also when I started going to meetings with others, getting some food in my system, and feeling better. It made me remember how I felt when I was sober and I wanted to find that again. When I was using, I had almost forgotten about that period. It seemed so far away that I believed it was unattainable. I finally had a tiny bit of hope.

I still didn't want to be in treatment because my mind was playing tricks on me and telling me that I should leave. But Tiffany kept pressuring me to clean myself up. I stayed even though the physical pain was immense. I had to break through the bondage of the past year of heavy heroin use. I was emaciated and had infections in both arms. I had trouble walking and moving in general because my body was torn up. Everything hurt. I had poor circulation in my arms because of my damaged veins. My joints cracked constantly. I felt the disease of addiction in my bones and it was excruciating.

I met with doctors and counselors who outlined a program of recovery. It was the same shit I heard during my first stay at Talbot Hall and I was annoyed to hear it again. I even saw some of the same addicts as before. We'd see each other and say, "Wow, you're here again too? Neither one of us got this thing right." This time through, I believed sobriety was much further away and my chances of recovery were much lower.

Once the drugs were out of my system, confusion set in. It was like coming out of amnesia. *Where have I been? What happened? How many years was I out there?* Nights were horrible. I woke up trembling in a bed soaked with sweat. I had using dreams that were so vivid and real that they made me believe I actually got high. When I was using, I lived in a dreamlike state outside of consciousness. Real dreams were so similar that I couldn't tell the difference between coming down from a high and waking up from sleep. In my using dreams while in treatment, I could sometimes feel the chemical reaction of the drugs in my body or taste the drugs in my mouth. I felt out of control and that was terrifying.

During the day, we were allowed to smoke in a sealed room. We sat around a table without talking to one another as we faced the consequences of our addictions. We shook and twitched as we smoked in our hospital gowns. Most of us didn't wear our own clothes. The homeless guys didn't have any clothes, and people like me showed up with a pair of jeans and a few shirts. We were there for ten days without laundry facilities, so we either had to wear the same clothes multiple times or start wearing the gowns and robes that were provided.

We were forced to eat and weren't allowed to leave the cafeteria until we did. The food was awful. It tasted fake to me, but I wasn't a good judge of flavor since I had lost my ability to taste. None of my bodily functions had returned yet. It was the first normal food I'd eaten in a long time. On Fridays, we ate pizza and that was exciting to me. It seemed like a miracle. I was still in survival mode and little things such as pizza and soda were important to me.

After medical detox, I was hit with a flood of emotions. Once the numbness of being high passed, I began crying all the time. *I hate myself.* I cried about my relationships with Mom, Dad, and my sisters. I cried about all of the problems I was afraid to face. I cried about the lack of dignity I felt at the treatment center. I was ashamed to be there. It was all very emotional, a tidal wave of sadness. It was also lonely. I didn't have any friends to whom I could reach out and talk. It was an important turning point for me when I started to embrace what they were teaching me at Talbot Hall and understand that I needed to become part of a community. I spent so many years isolated in my cave of addiction that I didn't believe I could have a deep connection with another human being.

Community was necessary in order for me to get sober. I tried to quit using on my own many times, and I was always doomed to fail. I usually made it to day three, which is the hardest day. If I could just make it through that, day four would be the easiest. Instead, I always went back to the dealer to buy more drugs on day three because my joints hurt and I felt like I was sick with the flu. I was vomiting and couldn't eat, had diarrhea, and alternating periods of chills and sweating. My blood pressure was high and I was constantly shaking and twitching. I sat at home wearing sweatpants and staring at the wall until I couldn't take it anymore. *I have to get high.* It was impossible to detox on my own.

Medical detox is still miserable and painful, but it alleviates some of the symptoms and doesn't feel like the flu. More importantly, I wasn't doing it alone. At home, there was no one to help me face the emotions that arose. In treatment, I could process those feelings during group therapy sessions. I needed to be held accountable because it was too easy to lie to myself about my addiction. In treatment, I was surrounded by people who called me out on my lies. It's exactly what I needed and it's why sobriety finally stuck for me. Less than two years passed between my stays in Talbot Hall, but it felt like at least a decade.

I'm in the IOP classroom sitting in a little desk that makes me feel like I'm back in school. "HOW" is written on the whiteboard at the front of the room. It's the twelve-step acronym for honesty, open-mindedness, and willingness. Rodney is wearing a dashiki. He's not a large man, but his spirit and enthusiasm fills the room. He's asking each of us to share what we're doing to get sober. "I'm trying to go to meetings, trying to get a sponsor, and trying to go through the steps," I say.

Rodney looks directly in my eyes, reaches into his pocket, throws his car keys on the ground and says, in a preacher like voice, "Try and pick those up son! You either do or don't. You either pick those damn keys up or you don't. You can't try and pick those up! You've either got to pick them up or you don't pick them up! That's how sobriety is. You either shit or get off the pot. You either do it all the way or you don't do it at all. There is no halfway. You can't do it halfway. You've got to be all in. The next time you come back here, I want to hear that you went to the meetings. I want to hear that you got a sponsor. I want to hear that you are working the steps, not that you tried."

There is so much power behind his voice and his message is clear. It's intense, but exactly what I need. Everyone in the room feels it.

"You either pick those fucking keys up, or you don't pick them up. If you don't pick them up, then just know that you're making the decision to step closer to your disease, instead of closer to sobriety."

For the first time, I feel like someone is actually telling me the truth about sobriety. The story in my head shifts from "I will try" to "I will go to a meeting." I don't have anything else to do besides go to IOP. I have no job. I have a wife at home who takes care of me. Here I am showing up at IOP saying that I'm trying to make it to a meeting.

Rodney's message makes things crystal clear to me. "What else do you have to do? You don't have anything to do. You can't get your lazy ass off the couch to go try and save yourself? We're throwing you a life vest and you just don't know it."

It reminds me of that story about a man who was stuck on his roof after a terrible flood. He asked God to save him, so God sent a person in a canoe, a person in a motor boat, and a person in a helicopter. The man refused to go with each one because he was waiting for God, so he drowned. When he got to heaven, God said, "I sent you three things. You wanted me to come down and pick you up?" My previous times in treatment were like the canoe, motor boat, and helicopter. Rodney was a miracle, a life raft who came to save my ass, even though I'd thrown away the other options.

Rodney makes it clear to me that I'm feeding him bullshit and he is going to continue to call me out on it instead of accept it. It's exactly what I need and it's making me think. Suddenly the clouds part and I know this is where I need to be. I can get sober again.

CHAPTER 13

ALL IN

After five days of detox, I was transferred to a room full of people who had some time in sobriety. It was an IOP meeting where I was surrounded by role models, people I could look up to because they were sober and really living the program of recovery. *I want to be like them.* It was a first for me. I finally felt like I was in treatment for the right reasons. I started to understand that I wanted sobriety and was willing to work for it. Rodney was a recovering crack addict turned counselor, and his "key" speech was a pivotal moment for me. It was like a light switched on. I was ready to fully invest myself in getting sober.

I heard similar messages eight hours each day during the month I spent in IOP. I remembered how good my life was during my first stint of sobriety and believed I could return to that through a program of recovery. I also realized that I hadn't been willing to do absolutely everything I needed to do in order to stay sober the first time around. There were five things necessary to stay sober—pray, attend meetings, create inventories, make amends, and constantly check in with my sponsor and support group. It's a lot of work, and I simply wasn't all in during my previous period of sobriety. But the final time I was out drinking and using, I was brought to my knees. I was humbled. I had to ask for help. I had to be willing to put myself out there because I needed help from others. I couldn't do it on my own. That was suddenly very clear to me.

Until then, I didn't fully comprehend what the first step of recovery is about. The first word is *we* instead of *I*. *We admitted that we were powerless over alcohol—that our lives had become unmanageable.* The first time I started the program, I would have replaced the *we* with *I*. I thought it was an individual thing. However, the second time through, I saw the *we* and realized that I had to do it with other people. I had to get a sponsor and ask for help. I also recognized that I met people when I was sober before who were still in my life and willing to help me. There were ten people to whom I felt very connected and with whom I was open to sharing. I reached out to each person and asked for help. "I want to get sober and I know I can't do it alone. I need your help." It was a huge step for me because it was the first time I had ever asked another human being for help. They all agreed to help me. We went to meetings together and spent lots of time together as sober support.

I found out that I needed to choose a new sponsor more carefully than I had chosen John the first time. It was important to find someone who had more time than me so he could be my guide through sobriety. I needed a sponsor to show me how to stay sober based on personal experience. I was told that I might hear someone say something that I really identified with at a meeting, or that

I would meet someone who had a lot of time in sobriety and had put a huge amount of work into himself. Then it would become clear that I wanted him to be my spiritual guide. It is a scary thing to ask for a sponsor because it requires a high level of vulnerability. "I need your help. I can't do this alone. Will you sponsor me?" Those are tough words to speak. It was difficult for me to ask for help because I had been beaten down so low. *I've gone too far. I can't be helped.* Those words went through my mind even though I desperately wanted to get sober.

The friends who supported me by going to meetings with me and taking care of me also helped me find my next sponsor. They said, "We want you to meet this guy named Raleigh. He's a smart guy who we think you'll like. We think he's your sponsor." Shortly after that conversation, the guys picked me up for a meeting one day and we stopped at a coffee shop on the way. Raleigh was sitting at a table when we walked in. It was a God moment as far as I'm concerned because my friends had no idea he would be there. After they pointed him out to me, I walked over and introduced myself. I discovered that Raleigh was a little rough around the edges, like me, and cussed as much as I did. I felt comfortable with him, so when I saw him at a meeting the following week, I asked him to be my sponsor.

Raleigh was an excellent sponsor. He was not my friend though. He was kind to me, but he was also very direct. That's how it's supposed to be. I needed someone who would always tell me the truth and who would cut right through all of my bullshit. Raleigh told me the truth at all costs because he knew it might save my life.

I began working through the steps with Raleigh, which meant surrendering control and giving myself over to a higher power I'd barely begun to understand. At four months sober, I reached the fourth step: *Made a searching and fearless moral inventory of ourselves.* When I made my inventory, I had to list all of the good and bad aspects of my character, all of my resentments, and all of the people who I had harmed. I wrote it all down on paper and it was a really big deal for me. I had one month to make a list of all the bad stuff I had ever done. It was a long list. That was hard enough, but the fifth step was even more difficult. I was told I had to share my list with someone, like my sponsor or maybe a priest. I had to be comfortable enough with the person to reveal all of the skeletons hidden in my closet. I chose to share my list with Raleigh because it seemed quite natural.

Raleigh and I went back to the same coffee shop where we first met. We sat down in a section with toys and books for kids because it was empty. It took me two hours to get through the list I had prepared. Soon after I began, people came in and filled some of the tables around us. I knew they could hear me, but I didn't care because I wanted to stop hating myself. I wanted to change. I was desperate to live. I wasn't interested in sharing my inventory in the first place, so once I started, I wasn't willing to stop because it would have given me an excuse to leave something out. I told Raleigh that I had to keep talking in order to stay sober. I continued to share the dark moments from my past, and some of the people around us eventually packed their things and left because of what they heard. I was willing to share what I needed to at that moment, and I wasn't going to stop just because other people shouldn't hear it or were going to judge me for it. My sobriety had become more important than anything else. That's the only way it can work.

When I went to my first meeting after sharing my inventory with Raleigh, everything changed. Before that, I had been doing all the right things, but hadn't passed the fifth step hurdle yet. I learned that most recovering addicts don't do the fifth step because it's so difficult. That's one reason why the success rate is only ten percent. Most people die from the disease of addiction. So when I showed up at the meeting and told everyone that I completed the fifth step, it felt like I had joined the group for the first time. Everyone stood up and hugged me. I still felt like a hopeless person, so being embraced by the group was exactly what I needed, especially after sharing my deepest and darkest secrets. It felt like the first estimable thing I had done for myself. I was proud that I made it past a step that most people don't clear. I also recognized that the weight of the items listed on my inventory had been bogging me down. Sharing them and letting them go gave me a sense of freedom. I suddenly understood that's what the program of recovery was offering me.

I had lived in isolation for so long that it was truly amazing to be embraced. I never felt like I fit into any group and was always trying to impress people. But the other recovering addicts in my group liked me despite what I had done. I received unconditional love. They told me, "We love you regardless. Thank you for showing up and doing what it takes to stay sober." Since my first drink, I had never felt so much a part of anything. I didn't want to be alone anymore.

My new sense of belonging kept me going as I continued to work through the steps. The eighth step involved making a list of all the people I had harmed, and the ninth step required that I make amends to each person directly. I didn't necessarily have to apologize, but I did have to make amends to everyone on my list, including Tiffany and my family. I'd had no contact with Mom or Dad for roughly two years. They were neither talking to me nor supporting me. They were just waiting for a phone call telling them that I was dead. I was very nervous when I had to make my amends to Dad. When I called him, he was happy to hear from me and relieved that I was sober. I talked to him at work the next day. I told him I wasn't there to ask for a job or anything else. I just wanted him to know that I was sober and willing to do anything necessary to make things right with him. Dad surprised me by saying, "We just lost our general manager and I think you might be the right fit for the job."

I replied, "I wasn't really here for that. I'll think about it and let you know."

Dad also said, "I want you to talk to your mom, your step-mom, and your sisters. I need you to make our family right again. Then I want you to talk to my partner Chuck as well."

I made amends to Chuck that same day. He responded graciously. Both he and Dad simply wanted me to be the best person I could be and to approach them without an inflated ego for once. I admitted my mistakes and they appreciated it.

The next weekend, I met with Mom and my sisters. They said, "We want you in our lives, but only if you're sober. You are an important part of this family." All they really needed to hear from me was that I was in recovery. They always loved me, but they weren't willing to enable my destruction. It took some time to feel like I was integrated back into the family. I was on guard with them because they knew how to push my buttons and I didn't want that to happen. I was still very fresh at sobriety and I'd been told that family could really throw me off track if I wasn't careful. It soon became apparent that the entire family missed me. When good things started happening, they wanted to be involved in my life again.

I continued to make amends to everyone and fess up to all of my bad behavior. I had to pay a couple of people back, but an honest conversation was the only thing I owed to most of the people on my list. Amends were difficult for me because I knew I had wronged people. I confronted each person and said what I needed to say without worrying about the response. I sat down with everyone I harmed, accepted what I did, and asked how I could make it right. It was tough, but I had to do it in order to free myself from my past and look into the eyes of society again. Feeling guilty about the past is poisonous and I had to let it go if I wanted to get healthy. My amends were not about receiving forgiveness from other people. They were about forgiving myself. They were for me. Once I owned my mistakes, I was able to stop thinking about them.

Even when the amends were rough, I experienced elation afterward. Making them gave me freedom. Freeing myself from the darkness of my past made me feel more alive than I had felt in years. My flame was starting to burn a little bit brighter each day. Health was slowly creeping back into my body and my soul. I still had a long and arduous road ahead of me, but I was gaining the strength to continue the journey. Most of that newfound strength was coming from my connections with other people. I was part of a recovery support group and I was a part of my family again. I felt like I was surrounded by a community for the first time in my life.

I'm driving away from the house I share with Tiffany for the last time. It's scary as hell because she was paying all the bills and taking care of me while I was getting high. It would be so much easier to say, "Let's figure this out." But I'm choosing a different path. I know that I have to live differently. Tiffany has been keeping me in the past and holding all of the things that I've done over my head. I've caused massive damage and I don't think the relationship can ever be repaired. My friends came over and loaded everything Tiffany would allow me take into my car. She flipped out the entire time. She didn't want to let me leave. Now I'm heading to a meeting because I have nowhere else to go. Although I'm scared, I feel good. I'm going on pure faith. I choose myself for the first time. I choose sobriety.

CHAPTER 14

A DIFFERENT PATH

I realized that my relationship with Tiffany was an obstacle to my sobriety because it was incredibly painful for both of us. She had been so focused on me when I was struggling that she didn't take care of herself and allowed her own issues to worsen. The more committed I became to sobriety, the further we grew apart. I went to several meetings a day for the first year. Tiffany wanted me to spend time with her instead. She said, "I helped you get sober, but you still don't spend any time with me because you're going to those goddamn meetings all the time!" We fought continuously about the new way that I was living. I had to prioritize my higher power and my sobriety before Tiffany. She was not happy about coming in third. I tried to explain that it was necessary for my recovery, but she couldn't understand that line of reasoning.

I knew I needed to divorce Tiffany for two reasons. First, I was going to file for bankruptcy and she didn't want her credit to be ruined. Everything we owned was in my name only, so she wanted to avoid responsibility for my unpaid bills. Second, she was angry about my sobriety. When I was using, Tiffany felt like she could control me. But once I was sober, she couldn't control me anymore because I had to take care of myself at all costs. Although my addiction was devastating for Tiffany, trying to save me gave her a purpose. It temporary filled the emptiness she felt inside. Without it, she was lost. We were lost.

I also realized that the damage I'd done to our relationship was irreparable. I destroyed Tiffany's trust in me. There was no easy fix for that. Trust can only be earned back, but I believed things had gone too far for that to be an option. I had also stolen Tiffany's sense of security and there was no way for me to repay that. It was impossible to quantify how much I had really taken from Tiffany because things like trust and security are intangible. I couldn't envision a way to make it up to her and she was not fully aware of how much I hurt her. She avoided acknowledging her pain, so I didn't know how to help her. Whenever I suggested that Tiffany get help for her own issues, she responded, "I don't have any issues. You've got the issues."

"Yes, but I did this to you and I want you to get well."

"It's all you. You are the problem," she would argue.

We went round and round like that with no resolution in sight. Tiffany wasn't interested in hearing my amends either. She was one of the first people on my list. When I attempted to make amends to her, she yelled, "You're not doing one of those fucking amends with me!"

I tried to explain, "I need to do it for you, but I also need to do it for myself. I need to clean up my side of the street." Tiffany wouldn't listen and the gulf between us widened.

After I finished IOP at six months sober, I told Tiffany I was moving out. She was irate and hurt, but I knew I couldn't let that stop me if I wanted to stay sober. The friends who embraced me at the meeting were the same guys who came over and helped me move. We were still going to meetings together and they were happy to help when I told them my relationship with Tiffany was jeopardizing my sobriety. They came over, acted as a buffer against Tiffany's anger, and put all of my things into my car. Then I drove away.

Later that day, I called Kris with despair in my voice and said, "I'm getting a divorce. My marriage is standing in the way of my sobriety. I have no place to stay."

He asked, "Are you still sober today?"

"Yes, I am."

"Today is a good day then. You can sleep on my couch."

I met Kris at a meeting and then followed him home. I was newly sober. I had no money. All I had was my car and the things that I packed inside of it. I knew the path forward was going to be very difficult.

I didn't realize it at the time, but the relationships I established during my first period of sobriety were what saved me the second time around. My support system was the only thing that allowed me to make it through the period surrounding my divorce with my sobriety intact. I felt like my whole world was crashing down around me as I faced the wreckage of my addiction. On top of my bankruptcy, divorce, and homelessness, I had to pay for my recklessness while I was drinking and using. My decision to trade guns for drugs came back to haunt me after one of the guns was used in a shooting and its ownership was traced back to me. Before I left Tiffany, ATF agents showed up at her office one day and demanded to speak to her.

"Where is your husband? A gun that is registered to him was used in a shooting last night. We don't think he was involved, but we need to know how that gun got into the shooter's hands."

I panicked when Tiffany called to chastise me for it. "I can't have you damaging my reputation at work like this," she said. I was mostly worried about the consequences I was going to pay though. *Holy crap. I'm going to jail for this. How could I have been so dumb?* I called a lawyer friend to ask for advice. He accompanied me to make sure I told the truth without incriminating myself when I sat down with the ATF agents and answered their questions. I knew I would likely be facing charges after the meeting, so I offered as much information as possible hoping for leniency. I told them that I didn't sell the guns for money; I traded them for drugs during my addiction. The agents wanted to know exactly which dealers to whom I gave guns. I tried to remember every detail of each deal. It was humiliating. *Wow. Why did I do that?* Of course I knew why I did it. I reached a point of no return and guns were the only valuable things I had left.

I think what happened next was another God moment because I was not charged with anything. The ATF just needed to know where each gun was and wanted to ensure that I didn't profit from them beyond trading them for drugs. When I walked out of the courthouse, I felt like God said, "You better stay sober because you could have paid a big consequence." A gun charge could have been up to fifteen years behind bars. Escaping all charges make it clear that I was being taken care of.

With my wife, possessions, and home stripped away, the only thing I had left was faith that it's never too late to change. When I left Tiffany, it would have been so easy to turn the car around and say, "Fuck it. I'm going to the bar." The last thing I ever want to do is say, "Fuck it." If those words come out of my mouth, it's dangerous. Sobriety is over at that point. I was really close to throwing it all away when everything was crashing down around me though. I was sad because I knew it was all my fault. I ruined my marriage, caused the bankruptcy, and gave guns to criminals. *Now I have to take responsibility for my actions and clean up my life.* It felt like a colossal task of picking up the pieces.

Living with Tiffany was going to make me drink again, but she wasn't the only person from whom I had to distance myself. *If I used or even just drank with you, I'm cutting ties and walking away.* I made a conscious decision to let go of many relationships. It was an incredibly difficult thing to do, but I knew it was necessary in order to save myself. Extracting myself from those relationships left me feeling alone. I had no idea what the future would hold for me and I was terrified.

I've been staying with my friends since I left Tiffany, and I don't want to become a burden. I need to find an apartment but I'm anxious about calling landlords. I'll have to ask them not to run a credit check. I'm only twenty-four years old, but there's no way I will pass because of the bankruptcy. I don't think they will rent to me. I'm sitting in my office chewing off my nails because I'm so nervous.

It's the end of the day and I finally work up the nerve to call about an apartment that looks good from the outside. The woman who answers says, "You can look at it. It's a little bit bigger than an efficiency with a smaller fridge. It's a nice place. We do run a credit check and there's a twenty-five dollar fee."

I meet her at the apartment the next day and she is very cool. I have so much guilt and shame about my bankruptcy that I feel sick to my stomach. I decide to be completely honest and up front with her. I lay it all out. "I'm in recovery. I'm trying to rebuild my life. I know I can afford the rent for this apartment, but I won't pass the credit check. I need a place to stay and I like it here. I will pay you. I promise to God I will pay you. I will never be late. Never."

I'm shocked when she says, "That's fine." She's not even the landlord; she's the property manager. She charges me twenty five dollars but doesn't run a credit check.

It's a miracle, but I still don't have any money and she's asking for fifteen hundred dollars up front. I don't know how I can come up with that. I'm making decent money at work, but my divorce cost me a lot. I need to borrow money, but I've destroyed all of my relationships. Everyone knows that addicts don't usually get sober and pay back loans.

At work, there is no other option but to ask Chuck, Dad's partner, for an advance. I walk down the hall and ask him for the money.

He replies, "I appreciate everything you're doing for us and I think you really need this." He rounds up when he writes the check so I have extra money to buy a couch. I pay the apartment manager and move in on Saturday. Another miracle.

CHAPTER 15

REBUILDING

I decided to accept the general manager position that Dad offered me because I had no other job prospects. I was surprised they wanted me back since I was not exactly a model employee during my addiction. I was never fully present and I stole time from the company by saying I was working when I really wasn't. But, they allowed me to start with a clean slate after I made amends. Then Dad's partner Chuck even gave me an advance when I asked him for fifteen hundred dollars to cover the deposit and first month's rent for an apartment. Maybe it wasn't that big of a deal to Chuck, but it was a very big deal for me. I wasn't being paid much money at work yet and I couldn't afford my car payment. I was still living at a friend's house rent free. When I left Tiffany, she only let me take my clothes and a few other personal things. She kept the majority of our possessions. I had almost nothing.

Although I lacked material possessions, I still had so much to be grateful for. The dilemma of how to find an apartment with a bankruptcy on my record turned out to be much simpler than I expected. When I told Chuck, "I know you're unsure about my ability to stay sober, but I really need some money for an apartment so I can get my life in order," he was willing to take a chance on me again.

For the next eight months, all I did was make sure I upheld my end of the bargain. I paid all of my bills. I was one hundred percent focused at work. I went to meetings, worked the steps, and really worked my ass off to stay sober and clean up my past. I also started a step study with eight other people who were new to the program. It was kind of like a book group where we studied the steps of recovery and different perspectives on them. We were all newly sober and working very hard to stay that way. We shared our trials and triumphs in sobriety. It was important to have that camaraderie. But not everyone made it. During the twelve weeks that we met, one person died from an overdose, one committed suicide, and another was shot and killed by the police. Shortly after the study ended, one more person died from complications related to the disease. Only five people in our group of nine survived.

It was extremely hard to lose those people. I felt like we were all in it together and were trying to be there for one another. Having to attend their funerals made me understand exactly how sad the disease of addiction is. It is a progressive, fatal, and terminal illness. I also realized that the fight to stay sober is constant. There is a common saying among the addicts I know: "While you're in a meeting, your disease is outside in the parking lot doing pushups. Be careful, because it will win. It will kill you if you don't take care of your sobriety." Even early on in my recovery, I had plenty of evidence proving the truth of that statement. I knew I had to do all of the right things or I would either end up in prison, an institution, or a casket. Those are the end points of addiction. I refused to accept one of those options for myself. Losing my friends strengthened my resolve to remain sober. *I want to live.*

The five of us who survived from the step study all became more committed to sobriety and to helping one another. There were only four apartments in my new building, and by the end of my first year living there, each one was occupied by a member of the step study group. My friend Kenny moved into the downstairs apartment a couple of months after me. Then Matt and Kevin moved in shortly after that. We spent most of our free time together helping each other stay sober. Many times I've heard people say that once a person joins a recovery support group, a community of people will spring up around him or her. It seemed miraculous to witness that community spring up around me, especially after being so alone for so long. My days of being a loner and feeling disconnected from others were behind me. *I have friends now.* Being surrounded by a recovery community, even at home, offered further proof that I was on the right path.

I walk into the small yellow practice room at the back of the yoga studio. I'm five minutes early for class, but everyone else is already here. Joanie's mat is horizontal at the front of the room and I lay out the mat I borrowed from the studio in one of the two vertical rows facing her. I see one other guy and six attractive girls wearing skin tight clothing. I'm wearing baggy red basketball shorts that hang below my knees and socks. No one else is wearing socks, but I don't take mine off. What am I doing here? I feel totally out of place. I can't believe I listened to my sponsor when he told me I should do this.

Joanie opens the class enthusiastically. This is her first ten week beginner's class after teacher training and she's excited about having eight students. I missed the first week, so I already feel like I have to catch up to everyone else. She leads us through half of the primary series and soon I'm sweating and struggling to catch my breath. I had a cigarette in the parking lot right before walking in here, so I'm having difficulty inhaling deeply like she instructs. I'm sure my face is as red as my shorts.

I'm far from being a picture of health. I'm sober, but I look sickly and gray. I have no muscle tone at all. I'm skinny, but soft and doughy. My body is not cooperating and I feel like I'm failing miserably at yoga already. I'm a competitive person and assumed I'd be able to walk in here and be good at yoga right away. How hard can it be? It's just stretching, right? This is so much harder than stretching. It's aerobic and my heart is pumping. I've been working out a little bit, but I'm not very active. And during my addiction I was completely inactive. All I ever did was sit in a chair and get high.

The girls in the class are kicking my ass. I'm embarrassed and feelings of self-loathing are creeping in. I should be able to do this stuff and I can't. I have to keep up with the girl next to me, but she's ridiculously flexible. I bet she's a dancer. She has an unfair advantage. I should be able to touch my own toes but I can't. Joanie teaches us chaturanga, which is a yoga push-up, and I can't do it. I'm not strong enough and I can feel all the places in my arms where I stuck needles. They hurt and I know the pain is going to be there for the rest of my life. I'm trying harder than anyone else in the class because I have to uphold the Hunt standard. I'm berating myself for not being good enough. I think yoga is a competition like golf and basketball. I'm driven and I won't give myself a break. I'm miserable.

The experience is unsettling because I can feel that something is going on inside of me. I feel vulnerable and uncomfortable. I'm immediately discounting everything that yoga is offering me because it is too much. It's like a mirror and I can see that I'm being competitive and that I'm angry about not being the best. This is new to me and so far outside my comfort zone. I'm glimpsing my true reflection and it's not the person I want to be. I have so much more work to do if I want to stay sober and clean up my life. Am I too far gone or can I become a better person? I don't know the answer.

I make it to the end of class and Joanie asks us to lie down, close our eyes, and take rest. I can't close my eyes.

"You need to close your eyes," Joanie says.

I don't do it because I want to get out of here as soon as possible. Fight or flight mentality kicks in. Yoga is providing me with a mirror and I don't like what I see. I can feel all of my assets and liabilities as I lie on my mat. How can yoga be working on me already? It's unsettling. Things are bubbling up inside me and making me anxious. I'm pissed that I feel this way. Plus, the way Joanie talks to us makes me believe that yoga is only for girls. I shouldn't be here. Tears of rage are in my eyes because I feel so raw. I get a sense of how powerful yoga really is. It scares me.

The rage grows in me until Joanie dismisses us. She's been standing near the door and can see my tears. Joanie tells me she'll reach out to me later because it's clear I don't want to stay and chat. I can't face any of the emotions I felt in here today. It would be so easy to use right now. I make a beeline out the studio door and into the parking lot where I *immediately light a cigarette. I'm never coming back to this place.*

CHAPTER 16

SHAKEN TO MY CORE

The early, honeymoon phase of sobriety is often referred to as the pink cloud because life is suddenly so much better. It is a period that feels wonderful but can be dangerous because it's kind of like looking at the world through a pair of rose-colored glasses. During that time, it seemed like everything was going my way. But everyone eventually has to step off the pink cloud and face the realities of life in recovery. When that happened to me, I realized that I still had a massive amount of work to do on myself and a huge amount of debt to pay off, both to the bank and to society. Additionally, I gained too much weight, got into a major car accident, and was bitten by a dog at the park. *Why are so many bad things happening to me now?* I felt like everything was crumbling around me. It was overwhelming.

I also began figuring out exactly what I needed to do in order to stay sober. In the beginning, I did every single thing that was prescribed by the program of recovery and my sponsor. That is the safest course. But each individual person eventually has to decide how much involvement in the program is necessary to maintain sobriety. Some people have to follow every suggestion without any wiggle room. Others can do the bare minimum. Most people are somewhere in the middle. I started playing around with the formula to discover what was right for me. I learned that I could go to meetings every other day instead of every day and still be alright. I had to find the right balance. Ideally, the program of recovery is not my life. It is meant to give me a life.

After I stepped off the pink cloud, I realized that I still had a low sense of self-worth and didn't like myself very much. I had further cleansing of the past to do. I needed to complete a more thorough assessment of my assets and liabilities so that I could gain a truer picture of myself. I needed to redouble my efforts in sobriety because I made it past the first significant hurdle, but there were many more hurdles to clear. *I'm sober but I don't think this is how my life is supposed to look. Something's still missing.* I had to keep working and changing. I was either growing or dying. I saw that there was no middle ground for me. I needed to keep evolving, and that is a process that will happen daily for the rest of my life.

As I came to terms with all of that, I continued working the steps and made the majority of my amends. I was developing more friendships. *Wow, people actually want to hang out with me now.* Life was improving, even if it was not always perfect. I was starting to feel good about myself. I was surrounded by awesome people. I was experiencing moments of happiness for the first time in years.

I took a turn toward spirituality when I reached step eleven. *Sought through prayer and meditation to improve our conscious contact with God as we understood Him, praying only for knowledge of His will for us and the power to carry that out.* I was very serious about that step. I got on my knees to pray every single morning for the first time in my life. I began studying religion as well. My sponsor told me I needed to explore different religions to determine what was right for me, so I did. I went to church. I got baptized. I studied Buddhism. I meditated. I studied Hinduism, Judaism, Sufism, and Islam. I read many books about all of the major religions and then asked myself what fit and what didn't fit. As a child, my family went to a non-denominational Christian church and that's all I had ever known. When I broadened my horizons, I began to understand that there are many paths to God. Ultimately, what impacted me the most was learning that interacting with others in a loving way is a common thread across all spiritual traditions. That's the standard I aspired to apply to my own life.

Although I didn't know it at the time, that spiritual work was foundational to the path that lay ahead of me. In early sobriety, I met Joanie, who became my first yoga teacher, despite my resistance. Joanie was also in recovery and I typically saw her at meetings about once a month. My impression of her was that she was deep into yoga. That's all she talked about and she was constantly attempting to recruit other people to try it. *Will she ever shut up about yoga?* I simply wasn't into it and I thought yoga was only for women. Joanie seemed very pushy when she asked me to attend her class. I said, "No, I'm not interested in doing your yoga. Leave me alone." I was feeling macho at the time and only wanted to work out at the gym so that I could get buff and sober at the same time. My ego was too big to accept the offer of yoga. *I wouldn't be good at it. I never want to do it.* I wasn't open to the possibility.

But I suddenly began running into Joanie more frequently and she continued to invite me to class. One week, I saw her six days in a row. *What the hell is going on?* On the sixth day, she said, "I think I'm supposed to be teaching yoga to you."

My response was, "Leave me alone about yoga. I'm not going to your class." I thought she was crazy. *What does she mean, she's supposed to be teaching me yoga? I'm not supposed to be doing yoga.* I was so disturbed by the interaction that I felt like I needed to call my sponsor.

"Raleigh, I keep seeing this woman everywhere I go. She keeps asking me to attend her yoga class and she's not hearing me say no."

Raleigh asked me, "What step are you on?"

"I'm on the eleventh step."

"Can you tell me what the eleventh step is?"

"It's sought through prayer and meditation to improve our conscious contact with God."

"Well, isn't yoga a form of meditation?"

"What do you mean?"

As always, Raleigh was brutally honest with me. "It's like you're not paying attention. God has opened up the yoga door for you. It looks like you're going to be doing some fucking yoga."

In disbelief, I replied, "Are you serious? I've changed so many other things in my life. Couldn't there be another way?"

Raleigh said, with certainty, "There is no other way. That's how you're going to find meditation. Tell Joanie you're going to do it." Then he abruptly hung up the phone.

"Shit. No way," I said as I hung up the phone. I tried to imagine myself going to yoga class. *What will I tell my friends?* I didn't know anyone else who did yoga and I certainly didn't think any men went to class. I didn't believe it was a socially acceptable activity for me.

When I saw Joanie at another meeting, I finally said, "Alright, I'll be there at one o'clock on Saturday. I'm not sure if I'll be any good."

In that first class, we did half of the primary series of Ashtanga yoga. It was a led class, which meant that everyone did the same poses at the same time. It was a very tough class and my body was out of shape. By the end, I was a hot, red, sweaty mess. Even though I got my ass handed to me, I liked the fact that it was so physically challenging. That's definitely not what I expected from yoga.

Being in that class brought many of my issues to the surface. I felt insecure and didn't think I was good enough. I was unfocused and checking out the attractive women around me. I was looking at the stinky guy next to me and judging him. It was a snapshot of where I was in life and in sobriety at that point, and I didn't like much of what I saw in myself. Despite that, the practice immediately made me feel real and alive in a way that I had never experienced before. It also brought me face to face with the present moment for the first time in my entire life. I was suddenly paying attention to the right here and the right now. I was very conscious of everything that was happening around me and inside of me.

It scared the shit out of me though. I didn't really think I would attend another class. It made me realize that I still hated myself, and I desperately wanted to stop feeling that way. I thought I was past it, but yoga made me understand that I wasn't. It shined a spotlight on my negative self-concept and that felt terrible. *I don't know if I'm ready for this.* I was already following the program of recovery closely and doing everything I believed I needed to do in order to stay sober. I was willing to change everything in my life, but I didn't feel ready for what yoga was offering me because it felt too powerful.

When we laid down to rest at the end of practice, I was sad and angry. *I'm not okay with this.* I was sweating badly and the sweat was mixing with tears and running down my face. My sweat was filmy because my body was in desperate need of detox. It was like oil pulling, extracting all the crap out of me. I'm certain I stunk as badly as the guy next to me. I felt absolutely gross. The sweat of the primary series worked to cleanse me. On that particular day, the cleansing was extensive. The poisons I had injected into my body were seeping out of every pore. I felt like I was placed directly into the fire of yoga to burn away the remnants of my past. It was a grueling, overwhelming experience and it frightened me.

I was so unsettled and pissed off that it would have been easy to walk right out of that class and buy some drugs. *I can't deal with all of this. I want to get high.* Instead, I turned to food. I had just done something that was really healthy for me and it made me tremble inside. So I ran back towards things that were unhealthy. I ate a huge amount of fast food, drank soda and an energy drink, and smoked a pack of cigarettes. *What just happened to me?* I had the rest of Saturday afternoon to contemplate that question.

After eating all of that food, I went home and zoned out in front of the TV for a few hours. I was trying to recover from being shaken to my core. I went to a meeting later that night and shared my experience with the group. I said, "I went to a yoga class today and I feel like it threatened my sobriety. It made me feel vulnerable. I don't know if it's a good thing or a bad thing. What should I do?" The consensus was that yoga was a powerful and important experience for me and I should go to another class.

I called Raleigh for another opinion and told him how I felt in the class. He laughed and said, "It sounds like you're telling me the yoga worked too good. Go back to class." Then he hung up the phone. I trusted his opinion and the opinions of the people in my support group. *It looks like I'm doing yoga again.*

I walk out of the studio after my second yoga class. It was powerful for me and different. I'm not trying to run away like the first time. I'm so grateful I listened to my sponsor and came back. I'm wearing the same clothes as before because these are the only shorts I have. It's a beautiful summer day and I'm stunned by the bright yellow sunflowers I see to the right of the door in the courtyard. They are gleaming like the sun. It's remarkable. I look around at the giant trees and feel like I can see the life pulsing through them. The bark is so brown and the leaves are so green. The green is overpowering. All of the colors are vibrant, but the green stands out because it's so deep and so alive. I've never seen anything like it. I notice the darkness of the mulch surrounding the trees, the gray of the concrete curb, the black of the asphalt parking lot, and the bright white of the parking lines. Wow, there's so much color here! It's profound.

I suddenly realize my whole life has been dulled and distracted, like I've been living in black and white. For how long? I can't remember ever seeing color like this before. But I didn't realize there was no color until today. It's not just *my sight either. I'm constantly turning up the volume on my music because my hearing has been dulled too. Why? Was it the drugs? Was it the isolation? Both? I didn't even know what I was missing. I guess it makes sense because I originally began using chemicals to hide from my feelings. Isolation and dulled senses were better than sadness. But today it feels like I have a new opportunity in the world.*

I can't get over the green. Holy crap! The trees are green? That's what green looks like? I've never seen this before. I've been so in my addiction that I've missed all of this. How sad is it that I didn't know the colors of the trees or the leaves before? The thought brings tears to my eyes. I'm so grateful that I'm sober and able to see these things today. I smile ear to ear as I continue to stare at the green. I can't look away. Now I can see it all. There's so much beauty everywhere. My mind is blown.

CHAPTER 17

SO MUCH BEAUTY

There was another week before the next yoga class and although I already knew I had to go back, I asked a few other friends for their opinions, hoping for a different answer. Yoga felt so good and so pure that I didn't know if I could do it. Every person I asked said some version of, "Taylor, you're trying to live differently and nothing happens by coincidence. Joanie walking into your life at the exact moment you're looking for ways to further free yourself from your disease is not a coincidence." None of them practiced yoga themselves, but they all believed it was something I needed to do. It felt like I had no choice. I was resisting because I was a little angry about that. It seemed to me as though the script had already been written and I didn't have a say in it.

I was trying to reform my personality and take stock of where I was at in sobriety. I was also trying to figure out who I wanted to be and what my life was supposed to look like after starting over. Yoga was not what I envisioned for myself. I thought Dad, by succeeding in the business world, provided the only example of how to live my life. I didn't know there were other options. It was a big shift for me to open myself to yoga. I was the only one in my family who was completely open to meditation and prayer. I didn't have a male yoga role model and that was scary for me.

I went back to Joanie's class the following Saturday and I experienced many of the same things, with a little less intensity. At least I knew what to expect, so I was prepared for the emotions. During the first class, I tried as hard as possible because I thought it was a competition. In the second class, I realized I didn't need to compete. I simply needed to try and do my best, whatever that looked like. That allowed me to feel more peaceful and comfortable during the practice. Yoga also felt a little more accessible to me. I could do a couple of poses that felt impossible to me the first time. *Maybe I'm not so bad at this after all.* I decided to surrender and accept yoga for what it was. *I just need to be present on my mat.* Opening myself to that kind of willingness had a profound effect on me.

I felt so many emotions. I was callous, and yoga made me feel like I was being cracked open. The practice was fracturing the stone casing I built around my heart, and it made me very uneasy. I felt clear, almost translucent, and I was uncomfortable with that. I understood that I was still holding onto past events that were more than a decade old. It was difficult for me to let go of my resentments. Suddenly my head and my heart were beginning to feel more open. I was allowing life and energy to flow through me for the first time. The translucence I felt meant that there was a pathway to release the old. I felt clear, open, and completely different.

The entire class was powerful for me, especially when we laid down to rest at the end. I felt as though someone was right next to me and whispered gently into my ear, "You're perfect just the way you are." That was one of the most transformative moments of my entire life because I was still so uncertain about who I was. I knew I wasn't the material things in my life like money and cars, but I didn't know what other options existed for self-identification. When I heard that voice, I began to cry because in my heart, I didn't believe I was perfect just the way I was. I thought I was permanently flawed and marked, like I wore a scarlet letter. I also assumed that no one would accept my new lifestyle because sobriety wasn't considered cool. And I was adding yoga into the mix, which seemed even less cool.

But hearing those words caused two things to shift inside of me. For the first time in my life, I felt like the grass was green on my side of the street. I had always been grasping for something else, but I suddenly saw value in what I already possessed. I was finally content with what I had. I also saw the intrinsic value inside of myself for the first time. In the past, I always attached conditions to finding happiness. *I will be happy if I have more money. I will be happy if I find a hot girlfriend.* In that instant, I understood that I already had what was required for happiness and that it was all internal instead of external. I was entirely absorbed in the moment on my mat. Tears streamed down my face as I realized I had never felt any value in myself. It was a moment that fundamentally altered my way of thinking and changed the course of my life.

As we rested on our mats at the end of class, I felt serenity and euphoria. When I got up from my mat, Joanie could see that something had shifted in me. She was smiling from ear to ear when I saw her standing at the door. Joanie said, "I know. I understand. That's why I want to introduce as many people as possible to yoga." The twelve steps alone are powerful and yoga alone is powerful, but the combination of the two is exponentially more powerful. Joanie knew that because she was living a life of both already. Joanie hugged me and said, "I'll see you next week." I asked her how I could practice more often, so she gave me a studio schedule and told me to attend more classes. *I'm going to do this.* I started practicing as much as I could, and I never looked back.

As an addict, I was so numb and shut down that my body stopped functioning. Although things were beginning to improve, I was far from being a pillar of health. My heart, lungs, and other organs were not working at optimum levels. I didn't notice that my vision was dulled, but when I walked out of the second yoga class, I saw color for the first time in years. It was only in that moment when I realized that drugs had made me unable to recognize colors. I wasn't paying attention and I wasn't present enough to see them. Even during the first year of sobriety, everything was still black and white. I viewed life through a muted filter. Suddenly seeing green that day amazed me. I'd already had a profound experience of understanding that I wanted what I had, and then I grasped that I'd been living with a veil over my eyes. It was like abruptly looking at the world with new vision. That was some pretty serious shit for one day.

I was emotional because I felt deep sadness about the way I had lived, drinking and partying but not paying attention to life. *How did I miss all of this?* The recovery literature says it takes a while for the fog of using to lift. Seeing color seemed like a part of the fog lifting for me. Perhaps yoga took me through the fog with a snap of the fingers that day. Being present to the here and now was a much different way of living than when I was drinking and using and wanting to be someone else. I was always wondering how I was going to get more drugs or thinking about how shitty I had been in the past. I continually had one foot in tomorrow and one foot in yesterday. But suddenly, I saw what was actually in front of me. My eyes were wide open instead of tightly shut.

It felt like grace. To me, grace is simply being able to get out of my own way enough to let a higher power direct my life. That surrender allows my life to be in full flow. I felt as though God hand delivered a new way of life to me. It was the path, the playbook to life, that I had always sought. *This is the way.* Before that, I always acted as my own worst enemy and never allowed myself to grow. I finally accepted that I needed to make changes and that adding yoga was going to be a part of that. My mind was no longer resisting. *I accept the path that's appearing before me.* I was being swept away by something that I didn't understand, but I was determined to keep going. My default setting during my addiction was to either go backwards or stay in the same place instead of moving forward. I was finally ready to move forward. The prayer I say every single morning is: *Let me get out of the way so that I can best serve you. Show me your will. My will sucks. I'll take yours today.* The message is, *show me your way.* That's what grace is for me—being open and clear enough to say, *this might not feel good at the moment, but if it's what I'm supposed to do, then I will do it.* I was finally prepared to surrender and allow something larger than me to direct my life. I finally found a way from darkness.

I'm a wiry 6'3" figure walking through the parking lot of the yoga studio. My shirt is off and I'm still sweaty. I can feel my heart beating through my neck as my carotid artery pumps. I just worked my ass off in a led primary class. Practicing in there today was a difficult experience, physically and emotionally. I felt myself shedding so many layers. As I hop into my car, I make a plan to drive straight home and melt into my bed. I can feel the pain in my arms as I drive. They hurt all the time and still bear the marks of heroin addiction. They are covered in needle scars from using them as human pincushions while I shot up as many as thirty times a day. I have permanent black lines as thick as cables running down my left forearm and across my elbow. My muscles are in a state of atrophy and I look frail, damaged.

I'm just over a year sober and crystal clear about the fact that I want to stay that way. My sponsor tells me that if I want a different life, I have to do different things. As part of my recovery, I've been exploring spirituality and religion. Now I get down on my knees every day and pray to something without even knowing what it is. I'm desperately doing whatever I need to do in order to maintain my sobriety, including yoga. I'm overwhelmed by the powerful effect that yoga is having on me. I'm trying to wrap my mind around all of this as I drive. I glance at my throbbing arms and remember the red, puffy, oozing mess that they used to be when they no longer functioned. When I was using, I had so many infections that I was continually on antibiotics and fighting a constant battle just to keep my arms. They were always cold because my veins were destroyed. But now my arms are changing. I realize that practicing yoga has already started to bring circulation and warmth back to them.

I walk into the sad looking efficiency apartment that I share with my dog, Diyo. There is no color except for the dirt on the carpet and the tan sheets that cover the windows. The single room is mostly unfurnished beyond a mattress that is laying on the floor. My only possessions after my divorce are a computer and a 50-inch TV. I know it's a bleak scene, but I'm happy here. I don't care that I have no stuff. The other three apartments in the building are filled with sober friends and I know this is where I'm supposed to be right now. I cook some food and prepare to relax and process everything that just happened on my yoga mat. As I lie down, there is something weird going on in my body, and I don't understand what it is. I am aware of every single scar in my arms, each place I stuck a needle. I can feel all of the pain that I caused myself and all of the damage that I did. I know I am in desperate need of more healing. I need physical *healing, of course, but I also need to be healed from the self-hate and darkness that is left over from my life as an addict.*

I notice something I'm not used to—a profound sense of calm. My arms are starting to burn and I can actually feel the blood running through them. I've been told that the yoga practice is meant to boil the blood and burn up the toxins. I'm not sure exactly what's happening, but I know it's significant. It feels like someone/something is physically removing each one of the needle scars from my arms. They are all being extracted, burned away. I can sense the energy of the practice inside of me. The old is being swept away and the light is finally outshining the darkness. I am being cracked open and shedding a powerful layer in the process. My being is starting to feel lighter and life is returning to my soul. I'm getting a glimpse of a new path being cleared in front of me. The damage is being undone. The pain is decreasing. I feel like my arms are back. I'm healing.

CHAPTER 18

HEALING

I knew yoga was going to be a path of healing for me, but I often felt out of place at the studio. I considered myself to be very different from everyone else because of my past. It was difficult to get to know other students because I couldn't talk to them about the major thing going on in my life, my struggle to remain sober. I never brought it up because anonymity is foundational to the program of recovery. I also believed the subject of addiction was simply too heavy a burden to dump on someone I was just beginning to get to know. I was consumed with battling my addiction, but I kept it a secret when I was in the yoga world. I didn't believe that anyone could possibly understand me.

To say that I didn't exactly fit in is an understatement. I felt uncertain and feared that I lacked direction. I had a hard-nosed determination to do everything necessary for sobriety. I was committed to praying, attending meetings, creating inventories, making amends, and constantly checking in with my sponsor and support group. But I still had a stranglehold on life. It was so good that I didn't want to let go of anything. I imagine it seemed to others like someone took me off the streets and put me directly into a yoga studio. I cussed more than the other yoga people, I felt a little grimier, and I didn't understand all of the yoga language or the teacher-student relationship. I was also very forward when I interacted with others. All of those qualities made me seem rough around the edges.

When I was using, I developed all sorts of behaviors that I was trying to leave behind. I had a loner mentality because I spent so much time lacking authentic connections to other humans. I had difficulty meeting people, sustaining conversations, and developing relationships. When I tried to interact with others, I felt nervous and searched for things to say. I was horrible at making small talk. I was clumsy with my words and I was unfamiliar with the news and most pop culture references. It felt like the world had passed me by while I was on drugs. For years, I'd either been hanging around unsavory characters or had been isolated in my cave of addiction.

Suddenly, I was being reintegrated into society. I'd moved from being held captive by my disease to being an active participant in life again. I lacked the social skills to develop meaningful relationships with other people. I was brash, forward, socially awkward, and difficult to talk to. I interacted in a weird, intense, and in-your-face way. The other addicts and alcoholics in my life understood my behavior, but no one else did, especially yoga people. They couldn't relate.

It was a much different crowd than I was used to. I think red flags appeared when they met me because I was so unlike them. I was sarcastic, aggressive, cussed even more than I do today, and constantly made inappropriate jokes. Yoga people found me to be weird. I breathed harshly and had an angry tone when I spoke. I was definitely outside the norm at the studio. Yoga was beginning to remove those qualities from my life, but I wasn't there yet. I think people in the yoga community had to raise their shields a bit to block the negative energy that was emanating from me.

I still had doubts about my ability to remain sober and about whether I should be doing yoga. Although I was striving toward, self-acceptance, I still experienced bouts of self-hate. I was just out of the woods of addiction and really struggling to get my shit together. I'd done many bad things and was still trying to clean up my mess. When I was drinking and using, I was not truthful with myself or others, so I was working to become more honest. I was also still grasping for things I didn't need in my life. I was only beginning to learn that I needed money but I didn't need to hoard it.

In yoga class, I was consciously trying to fit in and figure myself out. It was kind of like choosing a sponsor— I asked Raleigh to be my sponsor because I wanted what he had to offer. At first, I didn't think I wanted what the yoga people had. But I soon began to realize that they did have a lot to offer. They had a steadiness of mind that I admired. They also had compassion toward other human beings, which was new to me. When I was fighting for drugs, not telling the truth, and living on the fringes of society, I had no compassion. I was simply trying to get my high and all of the other things I believed I deserved. It was all ego driven and selfish.

I realized that people in the yoga community had open hearts. *Mine feels like it's encased in stone.* They showed me the power of vulnerability and convinced me to try becoming more vulnerable in my interactions with others and to do things that were outside my comfort zone. I also realized that people who practiced yoga had open minds, while I maintained a closed off perspective. They accepted people for who they really were and showed me that there are two sides to every issue. It wasn't all good over here and bad over there. They taught me some really powerful things about compassion and acceptance.

After practicing yoga for a few months, I noticed subtle changes in myself. I took the next step toward shedding a layer of the streets and became open enough to learn from someone else. Developing the humbleness I needed in order to be taught was a huge step for me. I also began letting go of my vulgarity and unhealthy eating habits. I got closer to accepting myself exactly as I was and grew more comfortable in my own skin. My yoga practice also taught me that we are all connected. That kind of openness helped me start accepting everyone else for exactly who they were as well.

In my first yoga classes, I felt like an outsider. *I'm not one of those people.* I felt welcomed by the yoga community, but my life experiences and outlook on life were different. As I got deeper into my yoga practice, I started to change. I let go of things that no longer served me and the focus of my life shifted so that I no longer felt like the enemy. *I can be a part of something. I am a part of this.* I didn't foresee that type of open mindedness developing in me, so it was a surprise. It was a long journey of dropping the outside layers away and becoming a truer version of myself. I dealt with my issues, got my ego in line, and straightened my priorities. Yoga right-sized me.

As my heart and mind opened, the Ashtanga practice continued to heal my body. In addition to the problems associated with my drug use, I was also in several car accidents. I was hurt badly in one of them, but I didn't call an ambulance or go to the hospital because I was afraid it would jeopardize my sobriety. I didn't want to repeat the aftermath of my motorcycle accident. I was in a great deal of pain, but I decided to deal with it so I wouldn't be offered any painkillers. Sobriety was my number one priority and I knew exactly how easy it was to relapse. I couldn't even use my left leg, but I knew that if I went to the emergency room, the chances were very high that I would be offered narcotics. On top of that, my collarbone still bothered me from the motorcycle accident. I had to spend a lot of time and effort bringing balance back to my body and restoring its health. In the yoga room, I could tell that the Ashtanga practice was designed to do just that.

The primary series really worked on me. It thoroughly cleaned me out and healed me. When I came to yoga, I looked sickly, as though I was recovering from an illness. I could barely lift myself with my arms. I had poor circulation because my veins were damaged. I had a black mark on my left arm where I'd put the needles, and I could feel scar tissue inside. My muscles were in a state of atrophy because my arms hadn't been used for anything but shooting up. They hurt badly after each class. When I told Joanie how much I was struggling, she advised me to stick with yoga and continue coming to class. *It's that easy? Yeah, right.*

In the beginning, I practiced so hard that I was bright red in the face and struggling to control my breath. I felt like I had to exert that degree of effort if I wanted to find the clarity of mind that I experienced in that second yoga class. Eventually, I had to start letting go of some of my hard-nosed determination though. When I first began practicing, I plowed through the poses at all costs. *Knees? Shoulders? It doesn't matter. I'll sacrifice my back too. It's all on the line today. Yoga is making me feel great.* I could feel positive things happening in my body and I was desperate to become healthy. *I want more of this.* But when I approached the practice without an open heart, an overwhelming drive took over. I was doing everything necessary to remain sober, so I thought I had to bring that same determination to my yoga practice.

I was so driven that I used yoga as a tool to beat myself up. I approached the practice in that way because I was afraid of sliding backward into a life of addiction. I was pushing myself, but what I really needed to do was simply show up on my mat each day and surrender to the practice. It took a good deal of time for me to recognize that I needed to stop chasing the benefits of yoga and that I needed to work smarter instead of harder. In the beginning, it was all about the poses for me. *I've got to figure these things out.* But that's not what's transformative about the practice. Transformation arises through steadiness of breath and concentrated focus.

The healing I experienced in my arms made me understand that life was returning to my body and soul. That was just one of many miracles during that period: finding an apartment despite my bankruptcy, receiving an advance from work, hearing "you're perfect just the way you are," and then feeling the needle scars being removed from my arms. *Holy shit. Life is getting good.* I interpreted all of those events as more validation that I was on the correct path. I was being healed on psychological, physical, and emotional levels concurrently. I was happy and determined to continue moving forward.

The program of recovery from addiction got me to a point where I felt like I was beginning to live a really good life. But yoga felt like it was actually adding life to my being. It was transforming me into a more honest, open-minded, and willing individual. Yoga made me feel better inside and out. It added meaning to my life, so I gave it all that I had in return. I held nothing back. I knew how important it was after only a couple of classes. It was a sudden change from skepticism to embracing all that yoga had to offer. I rearranged my schedule so that I could practice more and my priorities shifted so that I had more time for yoga. *This is what I'm supposed to be doing with my life.* For the longest time, I didn't know what I should be doing with my life and I felt lost. I spent some time in college, but I didn't finish because I wasn't engaged. I thought maybe I was supposed to follow in Dad's footsteps with the business, but that didn't feel right either. Suddenly I had some clarity. I felt like a new path, the path of yoga, was hand delivered to me. I was certain it was the correct path for me. My life finally had a purpose.

I'm at our teacher training graduation ceremony. I don't feel like a yoga teacher though. Not yet. I feel like I'm just a good student. I'm only two years into my yoga practice and I'm very uncertain about where this journey is leading me. I know teacher training has been a stepping stone for me, but I feel different from everyone else in my program.

We're sitting in a circle on the floor of the studio and I'm facing our three teachers, Linda, Marcia, and Martha. There were thirty of us in the beginning, but there are only twenty now. We're acknowledging how far we've all come and those who didn't make it through the program. People are crying and expressing gratitude. It's an emotional scene.

Each of us is given the opportunity to share with the group. As we're moving around the circle, my gut senses that some of the comments are not genuine. People are wearing masks that look like what they think a yoga teacher is supposed to be. They're not being real. I keep hearing the phrase "love and light" over and over. That doesn't resonate with me because I think yoga is much grittier than that and much more complicated. At least it has been for me.

It's my turn to share. "I never really felt like I fit in with you guys. Some of our conversations haven't felt relevant to my life. This yoga and teacher training has been about finding my own boundaries, my voice, and my path. Some of our training, like the book work and teaching in front of a class, came easily to me. But I felt like an outsider because my story is so different. You all seem like teachers, but I don't see myself as a teacher."

I'm honestly sharing what's going on inside. I tell them a little bit about my journey and explain that yoga has taken me out of the gutter, given me a sense of purpose, and resurrected the human being inside of me that was overtaken by the animal of my addiction. I'm done wearing a mask. As I speak, I understand that there is real power in just being me.

CHAPTER 19

SELF-ACCEPTANCE

After attending my second yoga class, I quickly developed a dedicated yoga practice. I got on my mat every day, no matter what else was going on in my life. I didn't know where the motivation was coming from. It felt like a gift. I never considered the possibility of becoming a yoga teacher until one day when I was driving to work at three o'clock in the morning. When I passed the exit sign that would take me from the interstate to the yoga studio, I had a moment when I thought, *One day, instead of going to work for Dad, I'll be going there at three o'clock in the morning. I'm going to teach a morning Mysore class. That will be my work.* The thought surprised me and I wondered if and how it was going to happen.

I continued to attend Joanie's classes and she helped me so much that I felt like she was my yoga mom. She knew that I was searching for something important through my Ashtanga practice and was happy to support me in finding it. What I hoped to find was peace of mind and comfort being in my own skin. *I need to accept myself and stop wanting to be someone else.* Joanie answered all of my questions, and if she didn't have an answer, she pointed me to someone else who did. Our relationship had a huge impact on my life. It was a new type of relationship with a female. I felt like Mom and many of the women I dated needed me to take care of them. Joanie didn't need anything from me. She simply wanted to help and believed that she was meant to be the person who pushed me toward yoga. She was a truly caring person and took me under her wing. Joanie was committed to both yoga and recovery, with over twenty years of sobriety, so she was a role model for me.

Joanie was middle-aged and highly disciplined. She took a great deal of care in selecting and preparing her food. That, in addition to yoga, was helping her body heal while she devoted herself to recovery. Joanie taught yoga, waited tables, and strived for simplicity. She lived well below her means because she was saving for her first trip to study yoga in India. I began spending most of my free time with her. We were practice partners and I frequently ate meals at her house. We attended meetings, kirtan, and meditation sessions together. Joanie was continually pushing her own boundaries and was the catalyst for change in many others, including me. She opened the door to yoga for me and invited me to walk through it.

During the second summer of my yoga practice, Joanie was recruiting students for the teacher training program at the studio. The training was scheduled to take place at nine o'clock every Monday morning for nine months. She asked me to sign up for it.

I said, "I can't do that. First of all, I'm not going to be a yoga teacher. Second, even if I was going to teach, I'm not ready for that yet. Third, I work at nine o'clock on Monday mornings, so it's impossible. Who can do that? Soccer moms? I would enroll in the training if it was on Thursday evenings instead." I thought my excuses were airtight.

My conversation with Joanie occurred on a Monday. When I arrived for class on Tuesday, I saw an announcement on the bulletin board that said yoga teacher training would start in September and would be held every Thursday evening from six until nine, plus weekends. I asked Joanie about the schedule change and she assured me that she didn't ask the studio owners to move the training to Thursday evenings. *What the hell? How did that happen?* I already felt like I was living in a period of grace, and the opportunity to learn how to teach reaffirmed that for me. Just a day after I stated out loud that I could never do the training because I had to work with Dad, the schedule was changed. It felt like another God moment. A door was being opened for me just like when Joanie invited me to her class. I was being moved in the direction of becoming a teacher. I knew exactly what Raleigh would say if I asked him about it. I realized I couldn't say no.

When I filled out the application to be accepted into the program, I had to answer questions about why I wanted to be a teacher and what yoga had done for me. Two years of experience were required, but I'd only been practicing for about a year and a half. When I handed my completed application to Martha, one of the studio partners, I told her, "I don't have enough experience based on your requirements. Let me know if that's okay with you or not."

Martha quickly read over my answers and said, "Yoga has done all of this for you? You're in. We'll give you a pass on how long you've been a student."

So I signed up, even though I didn't have enough money for tuition. I put it all on my credit card, which had a ridiculously high interest rate thanks to my bankruptcy. I showed up for the first day of teacher training believing I had very little yoga experience, which was true. However, I was the only one who had a consistent daily yoga practice. Many of the other students dabbled in a variety of styles and didn't share my intense focus on Ashtanga. I believed that Ashtanga was the correct practice for me and I wasn't interested in trying out any other types of yoga. That was another reason I felt like an outsider instead of part of the group in teacher training. I didn't quite fit into the group and I felt misunderstood.

I gave the training all that I had though, and I felt like those nine months transformed me into a much better student. When they gave me a reading list, I thought to myself, *I've already read all of those books.* When we covered anatomy, I realized I'd already studied what I needed to learn on my own. I did everything possible to set myself up for becoming a knowledgeable teacher in the future, even though I wasn't yet certain I was going to teach. By the second half of the training, I felt very solid. The practicums came easily to me. I didn't mind speaking in front of people, and my voice was strong. It became clear to me that I was supposed to share yoga with others. I was getting better and better at it. Again, I surprised myself. *Holy crap. Maybe I am going to be teacher.*

That was a significant life change to wrap my mind around, and it wasn't the only one I experienced. About three months into teacher training, when I was still working hard at sobriety, I met Jessica. Some of my sober buddies and I were having a guys' night that ended at a late evening meeting in a different part of the city than where we usually attended. When we walked in a few minutes early, I spotted the hottest woman I had ever seen in the recovery community. She was tan with bright blonde hair and a beautiful face. She was wearing tight jeans with a white sweater and all of the guys were checking her out. I couldn't take my eyes off of her. At the beginning of the meeting, we introduced ourselves and shook hands with one another. I took advantage of the opportunity to talk to her. I learned that her name was Jess and that she was the chairperson of that group. I immediately decided to become a member of that home group so I could get to know her. My home group meetings were the ones I never missed and where I knew everyone. I checked in regularly because it kept me accountable. Jess was all I could think about during the meeting. At the end, we held hands and said the Lord's Prayer. I didn't close my eyes or say the prayer. Instead, I just admired Jess.

At twenty-two, Jess was four years younger than me and had just about one year of sobriety. She looked like an all-American girl and I guessed that she didn't have that low of a bottom. *She was probably only a light drinker who went down the wrong path. I bet her story isn't that hard and she hasn't lost as much as I have.* It's easy to discount younger people who are getting sober because they have shorter life experiences. But I would later learn that Jess's story is pretty rough too and she wasn't a good girl in the way that I assumed she was based on her looks.

I wanted to get to know Jess, but I thought she was out of my league. We hung out in the same circles, and I learned she was dating another guy in recovery who wasn't serious about sobriety. I avoided him because I was making an effort to surround myself only with people who were positive impacts on my life and committed to recovery. Jess and I socialized and got to know each other through our mutual friends over a two-month period. Neither one of us had much else to do in our newly sober lives. As I spent more time with Jess, I learned that she was quiet and reserved with a bad ass attitude. But I could also see that there was a very soft and kind person behind the external rock that she presented to the world.

Jess broke up with her boyfriend because he started using again, so I decided to ask her out. When I invited her to a Cincinnati Bengals game, she said no because she needed time to get over the break up. I had never been turned down for a date before, so I became even more intrigued by Jess. I sent her a text message saying, "Let me know if things change for you, because I would love to go out on a date with you."

She replied, "I need to figure some things out right now. If an opportunity presents itself later, we can go out."

I respected her wishes and didn't pursue her any further for a while after that. I didn't want to spend too much time on someone who had just told me no. I knew we would get together if it was supposed to happen. We still saw each other socially in groups on occasion and we were cordial with each other. I had no expectation that anything would happen between us. I waited patiently until a friend of Jess told me I should ask her out again. Jess had always been a little standoffish, but the next time I saw her, she seemed friendlier and suggested that we get together sometime. I decided to invite her to an Ohio State basketball game. I would soon learn that Jess hates sports, but she accepted anyway and we had fun together.

Since that was a group outing, I hoped she would join me on a real first date. I called Jess and said, "Valentine's Day is coming up soon. Would you like to go out to dinner with me?"

Jess said, "I would love to."

I told her to, "Pick a restaurant. We can go anywhere you want—the nicest place in the city or fast food. It doesn't matter to me. I just want you to choose." I found out that Jess was very indecisive and unsure of herself. It took her a long time to figure out where she wanted to go. When she picked a low key restaurant, I was relieved because I knew she wasn't high maintenance. We joke about her selection today, because now she would choose a much fancier place. But back then, she thought it was a big deal that we were going to dinner because of her life circumstances. Jess had never felt taken care of in the way that she's felt cared for in our relationship. She never thought she deserved to be respected, so she chose guys who treated her like shit. It would have been a big deal for one of the other guys she dated to take her out, but it was normal for me. I was used to eating at nice restaurants because part of my sales job was to have dinner with customers. Jess had dated other men who were just as shady as I had been when I was using. As addicts, we tended to attract people who were mirrors of ourselves.

Our dinner date went well. *How did this happen to me? I really like this girl.* I found myself getting more and more into Jess because the more I got to know her, the more she had to say. Jess is quiet and keeps things to herself, and at first, I read her as distant and guarded. I wasn't sure it could work out between us because she entered the relationship with her own baggage. Jess was still cleaning up her past and trying to get healthy, just like I was. And I initially couldn't pry enough information out of her to feel like there was any depth to our relationship. Our conversations often felt superficial compared to the deep work I was doing in my yoga practice. Eventually Jess began to let her guard down with me though. There were a few times when she opened up and told me exactly who she was and what she wanted to do with her life. *Maybe things will work out with her.* As her trust in me grew, she shared more of herself with me. When I saw Jess become open and reveal what she believed were her inadequacies, I understood that her true self had just been clouded by her addiction. I already knew that Jess is beautiful on the outside, and I soon was able to see what an incredibly sweet and beautiful person she is inside.

Jess and I quickly started spending all of our free time together. Within a couple of months, I was living at her house. We started taking vacations together and learning as much as possible about each other. As we grew closer, Jess told me, "The reason I was so intimidated to talk to you was because I could tell you were a good person. Most of the guys I knew were dishonest. I knew you had the right motives; you were simple, straightforward, and didn't lie. I thought you were too good for me to date." *If she knew some of my stories, she wouldn't think that about me.* Even though my self-concept was improving, her impression of me was still very different from how I saw myself. I felt like I still had a lot of work to do on myself.

Jess didn't feel that in me though; she felt my heart. She believed she was bad in the same way I thought I was bad, but it wasn't actually about being morally good or bad. It was more about being sick or healthy. We were both working on ourselves and trying to get healthy.

Jess always told me the truth from the very beginning. One of the most powerful things about our relationship is that she supported all my spiritual pursuits. I was diving really deep into yoga, chanting, and meditation. Jess wasn't always interested in participating, but she never stood in the way of me doing any of it. I thought it was a very important and positive thing for me to have a supportive partner on my yoga journey.

I never knew what intimacy was until I got to know Jess as deeply as I know her and allowed her to know me completely as well. I had never known anyone in that way. Our love really grew out of yoga and the commitment to my program of recovery. My love for Jess is a reflection of my love for myself. I wasn't able to truly love anyone until I could accept who I am to the core. Yoga helped me learn to love myself. Self-love flowed into my love for Jess and it felt clear and clean. I had never experienced anything so pure.

Self-confidence also allowed me to love Jess, and the Ashtanga practice was giving me the confidence to believe I could be the kind of man she deserved. She actually attended the first class I ever taught. It was also her first yoga class. I got the opportunity to teach through the House of Hope, a sober house and treatment center that was connected to the prison system. I had been attending meetings there and knew the director. The House of Hope was known as the last house on the block. It helped hardened criminals who lost everything and had no other place to turn. The director knew I was looking for yoga students, so he said, "I'll arrange a class and you can teach those guys."

The twelfth step of the program is: *Having had a spiritual awakening as a result of these steps, we tried to carry this message to alcoholics and to practice these principles in all our affairs.* When I reached that stage in my recovery, it became my responsibility to share my experience with struggling alcoholics and offer them a program of recovery. I couldn't keep the gift of sobriety unless I was willing to give it away by helping the next person in return. I think it may be the most important step, even though they are all very important.

I realized that teaching the class would be my twelfth step work. I also knew it was the perfect opportunity to get the practice hours I needed for my training program, so I asked for time on the studio schedule to teach it. I had fifteen students in the Sunday afternoon class. They included twelve hardened criminals from the House of Hope, a friend who also needed yoga teaching hours, along with Jess and her mom. I surveyed the room and thought, *holy shit. This is how I'm going to give back, how I'm going to share the message. I'll teach others who are in recovery. I'll be teaching them in a Mysore class one day.* My path was becoming even clearer.

The House of Hope students had recently been in prison where their only physical activity was weightlifting, so some of them were extremely muscular. They were stiff and yoga was physically tough for them because life had beaten them down. It was also very emotional. Whether they cried, became angry, or experienced some other emotion, it was important for me to simply hold the space and be present for them. They were all between two weeks and four months sober, so the experience was raw and intense all around. But they were committed to it and attended every week. Yoga wouldn't have been their first choice of activity, but they were glad to get out of the house and they were receptive to my teaching since they knew I was in recovery too.

It was a positive first teaching experience, but it was also difficult in the way that many of my interactions with other recovering addicts were difficult. Four of the twelve students died within the year. One left the household during our ten-week class, and three more passed away shortly after the class ended. Those types of experiences always make me realize exactly how lucky I am. *I just have to keep going, continue doing everything for my sobriety and for the next person.* I had made an enormous leap. In my addiction, I didn't care about anyone else. Yoga made me want to help others even more, and teaching that class made me clearer about my path. I saw people who'd been in prison having physical, mental, and emotional breakthroughs. It was exciting to teach my own class and it felt comfortable. *I am good at this.* It felt like something I was supposed to be doing and it was fun.

I arrive at Joanie's house to practice with Laruga. She's just back from studying yoga in India. Laruga teaches Joanie, Christian, and me on Monday, Wednesday, and Friday, and I pay her to teach me privately on Tuesday and Thursday. The first time I met Laruga, I immediately knew she was different than any other yoga teacher I had encountered. She is a very pretty, petite woman with curly brown hair. She's soft-spoken, thoughtful, and detailed, but there is an edge to her voice. Laruga practices with an intensity that really resonates with me. She is completely focused, tries incredibly hard, and is happy while doing it.

In Laruga's presence, I feel like I am being steeped in the tradition of Ashtanga yoga for the first time. I realize I didn't even know what Ashtanga was before Laruga came into my life. No one I practiced with knew. We thought we knew, but we didn't. She's giving me so much substance. Yoga suddenly feels like a spiritual path instead of merely a fitness class. At the studio, the teachers were instructing me through a stretching routine. Laruga is not instructing me through a routine. She is teaching me what the tradition is. This method is so different and so much richer.

After class, I follow Laruga outside to talk. I tell her everything. "Now I know how it feels to have a teacher. I see the huge amount of love and respect that you hold for this lineage. I don't understand it completely, but it speaks to me in a really deep way." I just want her to know that I'm willing to learn all that she has to teach me. I'm willing to follow her, and I don't follow very often. I'm at the point in my sobriety and practice when I need a guide and she has entered my life in exactly the right moment.

CHAPTER 20

IMMERSED IN TRADITION

I was in the process of learning that Ashtanga is a style of yoga that is based on a traditional method of teaching and is transmitted to students through an unbroken lineage of teachers. Many students travel to Mysore, India to study with R. Sharath Jois, the grandson of Shri. K. Pattabhi Jois, who taught yoga for more than seventy years before his death in 2009. Pattabhi Jois is affectionately referred to as Guruji by students of Ashtanga yoga. He established the Ashtanga Yoga Institute, where Sharath teaches today. Some students who study with Sharath in Mysore become authorized, which means they are given his blessing to teach others in their home countries. In Indian culture, this is known as parampara, which means a succession of teachers.

When I first began practicing Ashtanga in Columbus, the community was not very traditional. I had learned much from Joanie, but I didn't yet have a teacher who had been to Mysore and was connected to the lineage. That's why meeting Laruga was such an important turning point for me. She was only thirty and had already made several trips to study in Mysore. When I was with her, I could feel that she was immersed in the tradition of Ashtanga yoga. I immediately knew she was supposed to be one of my guides.

I encountered Laruga near the end of my teacher training because she was temporarily living at Joanie's house while she waited for her Swedish citizenship to be approved. She planned to move there with her boyfriend. I wanted to learn from her, but she didn't have a Mysore program because none of the local studios would let her teach since she was planning to leave soon. I wasn't really feeling the vibe at the studio anymore, so I was looking for a new place to practice. When I told that to Laruga, she said, "Come practice with me."

Joanie cleared out all of the furniture from her living room so Laruga could teach a Mysore class in there on Mondays, Wednesdays, and Fridays. There were never more than three or four people in the class, so she was able to give each of us a huge amount of detail and attention as she taught. It was intense, but so different from the way I had been learning yoga that I wanted to spend as much time with Laruga as possible. I asked her if she would teach me privately. She told me I could attend the group class three days each week and then if I paid her twenty dollars a day, she would teach me privately on Tuesdays and Thursdays. *Done deal!* I still didn't have much money, but Laruga's teaching spoke to me so clearly that I knew I could find a way to pay her. I was excited to be her student. *When the student is ready, the teacher will appear.*

Laruga was teaching Mysore style, which is different from many classes in the U.S. where the teacher creates a sequence of poses and leads everyone through them at the same time. The Ashtanga system comprises six series of asanas, or poses, which are taught in the same order to each student. Students are given the next pose by the teacher only after they can do the previous pose, so everyone's practice looks a little bit different. In a Mysore room, students practice at their own pace while the teacher assists each person individually. It's private instruction in a group setting. For someone who is new to the practice, a Mysore room can look a bit chaotic, but it's a highly effective way to tailor the yoga practice to each individual student. The practice is meant to be done six days each week, with one day off for rest.

The first series of poses is called the primary series. I had already been practicing the entire series when I began learning from Laruga. But what was different about her teaching is that she stopped me at poses if I couldn't do them properly. "You can't go on until you can do this one," she would tell me. She didn't allow me to practice the whole series right away. I didn't like being stopped at poses I couldn't do, so the effort I put into my practice became even greater. I had intensity and discipline before, but not enough to make me figure out how to achieve the difficult postures. Laruga's style of teaching made me realize I had to figure out every single pose before I could move on. That was a totally different experience than being offered a modification for a pose that was challenging. It made sense to me because it encouraged me to be more intelligent in my practice and to try harder on the things that didn't come naturally to me. I also realized that in order to become a teacher myself, I had to understand all of the poses.

Previously, I had been taught to skip or modify the postures that were difficult for me. Laruga helped me understand that practicing in that manner lacked depth and understanding. Today, I'm inclined to say that the practice is actually contained in the hardest poses. If I only do the poses that come easily to me, I will never move forward. The struggle with difficulty is what translates into the rest of my life. That struggle only occurs when I'm met with something I am unable to handle. The poses that initially seem impossible have taught me the most. *I need to be focused. I'm supposed to be aware of my breath. I just have to work at it. Every day I get better.* It's not a revolutionary idea; it's a very solid method of learning. For me, the beauty is in the struggle. Avoiding the difficult postures is trying to obtain the beauty without the struggle.

A Mysore teacher physically assists students when they are struggling with a pose or when it might be beneficial to help them go more deeply into a posture. Laruga used to push and pull to get me into poses. Her adjustments were smart and helpful. She was very detail oriented and didn't allow any part of my practice to be sloppy. My hand position, shoulders, the way I grabbed my toes—it all had to be perfect in her class. During the six months I practiced with Laruga, I learned more about Ashtanga than I had learned in the previous two years. That amount of focused energy directed at my practice made it explode. I completed the primary series with her and made a lot of progress toward further healing my body.

Laruga had a drive that was similar to my own. She believed in giving all that she had on her mat every single day, and she pushed me to my edge during each class. She also spoke to me with complete honesty, similar to my sponsor. She told me, "Taylor, you're really rough around the edges. Move on from your past. Let go of the addiction. Just be here right now." Laruga was never afraid to say the things I needed to hear, and at the end of the day, she didn't care if I liked her or not. She made me understand that is a characteristic of a good teacher. She was really teaching me instead of trying to be my friend. Laruga often said, "You're doing this pose today, or you're not going home. We're staying here until you figure it out." It was a new kind of learning experience for me and it was such a gift.

Laruga was the perfect role model for me as I was studying how to become a teacher myself. She was my first example of how to be a demanding teacher who pushes people through their perceived limits. Laruga expected a lot and gave a lot to her students in return. She appeared at the exact moment I needed her. Laruga embodied the tradition of Ashtanga yoga in a way that I greatly admired. She was the kind of person I hoped to be, both as a yoga practitioner and as a sober person. The feeling I got from the yoga community was not very different from that of the recovery community. They are both about living openly and honestly and being compassionate and empathetic toward others. Laruga taught me the tradition of Ashtanga, how to take myself less seriously, how to live nonviolently and truthfully, and how to avoid grasping for things. I could see that she applied those principles to her entire life. There were no mixed messages from her. How she practiced and how she lived were one in the same.

When Laruga was my teacher, she was living out of a suitcase at Joanie's house. That's all she had. I was struggling to obtain material things and pay my rent at the time I saw her actively searching for truth and simplicity.

Observing her made me realize that the relationship I had with my car, clothing, and other material possessions was not important. It was the first time I consciously realized that truth. I had moved from having many nice things to losing it all during my addiction, and then accumulating material goods again in recovery, to understanding that I didn't need any of it. Before Laruga, all of the people who I looked up to had fancy cars and nice houses. I was always striving for more because I thought that's what success looked like. *Give me more money. Give me fancier cars.* I was finally starting to move away from that mentality. For me, Laruga was a perfect example of how to live within my means and be happy with having nothing that I didn't really need. She was whole without any of it. I saw how material things got in the way and were a distraction from personal growth. I was blessed to learn that lesson from her.

As I grew in my yoga practice, my relationship with Jess flourished. After dating for about a year, we found out she was pregnant with Makayla. Although her pregnancy was a surprise for both of us, it was a God moment in my mind. Jess had severe endometriosis, her periods were excruciatingly painful, and she needed medical treatment for the condition. At nineteen, she had surgery and then six months of shots that caused her to experience menopause-like symptoms. She was only twenty three and on birth control so strong that it made her sick. She hadn't menstruated naturally in several years. One day Jess sat down with me and said, "I don't think this birth control is good for me. I feel like I'm dying on the inside. Should I stop taking it?"

Yoga had already taught me the importance of listening to our bodies, so I responded, "Of course. Follow what your body is telling you to do." Jess had started doing a little yoga, but she was suspicious of it and didn't believe in the practice the way I did. Still, she and I could both see the toll the medication was taking on her health.

Jess was upset when she revealed to me, "The doctor said it might be very difficult for me to get pregnant in the future."

I assured her that was alright. I honestly hadn't ever contemplated having kids, so it wasn't a big deal to me. I told her, "We can confront that issue later. There are other options, like adoption. Or maybe we're a couple who is not supposed to have kids."

Jess stopped the birth control and just six weeks later, we learned she was pregnant. I was a bit taken aback by the news at first, but my attitude toward everything at that point was, *if that's what is supposed to happen, I'm not going to fight it. Let it happen. Be witness to it.* I had let go of the belief that I needed to orchestrate the show. It seemed like a miracle that Jess got pregnant immediately after the doctor told her it wasn't possible, especially after taking the medication for so long. The message was clear to me that we were supposed to have a child together.

Jess and I began to imagine ourselves as parents and plan for the future over the next several months. Then, about halfway through the pregnancy, we received a scare when test results showed that Makayla might have Down syndrome based on the chromosomal reading. I had to take a few breaths and remember the journey that brought me to that point. I had done plenty of bad things and burned many bridges, so if that was the card that was dealt to me,

I was going to be okay with it. I didn't believe the two things were necessarily related, but I was willing to accept whatever happened in my life. We were worried about something that wasn't even a fact yet. *I'm lucky to be alive today. Remembering that I was at the edge of death a couple of times brings everything back into focus. I will love my child no matter what.* Jess was still very afraid, so we got down on our knees beside our bed and said a prayer together for the first time. Our fears did not come true, but our relationship was strengthened through that experience.

Before Makayla was born, Laruga was granted Swedish citizenship and left Columbus. That was a sad time for me because her absence left a hole in my life. Laruga taught me so much, and, without her, I was back to trying to figure things out on my own. *What am I supposed to do?* I was still teaching the guys from the House of Hope and I felt like I was becoming a better teacher and finding my voice. And my practice was much stronger after learning from Laruga. I still needed a guide though. Going in, I knew she would be leaving. I was happy for her, but it was still difficult for me as a student. I needed a teacher in my life as much as I needed a sponsor.

It's Sunday, my first day of practice with Matthew in Michigan. I've driven three hours to study with him. The experience is really deep. I finish and introduce myself. If I'm going to spend a week here, I want to get to know who Matthew is as a teacher. I can already tell that he is highly practical and very grounded.

"Can we meet for coffee?"

He agrees and we head to the nearest coffee shop. Matthew is tall and lanky with long hair and glasses. He wears socks in the Mysore room and plays the harmonium at the end of class on Sundays. His playing was beautiful today and it brought tears to my eyes. When we sit, Matthew begins to tell me a little bit of his own story. He speaks very plainly and seems more grounded than any person I've ever met. He explains that, "Yoga attracts crazy people and it attracts healthy people."

"Yeah, I know that. I was one of the crazy people."

Out of nowhere, Matthew asks, "Are you in recovery?"

I'm floored. "Yes, I'm in recovery. I've been sober for a few years."

I find out Matthew has much more time than me, twenty-five years. He invites me to a meeting that night. I feel like God has just given me another guide and is saying, "You were supposed to make this journey." I can't believe that I've chosen an Ashtanga teacher who is also in recovery. I also can't believe that Matthew is sharing such a serious secret with me on the first day. I would have felt too much guilt to do that. But I don't feel any shame or guilt coming from Matthew. He is simply sharing.

CHAPTER 21

ANOTHER GUIDE

After Laruga left, I practiced by myself each day after work. Jess was kind enough to turn our extra bedroom into practice space for me. I was still dedicated and worked hard at my practice, but it was so much different than having a teacher. I felt isolated and didn't enjoy having to figure everything out on my own again. I had to keep moving forward though. Yoga was giving me so much clarity. *You asked for a purpose. This is your purpose. Follow your path.* It gave me even more clarity than the twelve-step program did. The steps helped me clean up the street and then yoga was the vehicle that transported me down the street. Both of them were highly important, but yoga meant so much to me because it gave me direction. I spent such a long time feeling like a piece of shit that glimpsing another way of life transformed my self-concept and outlook. I was finally out of my own way and in the flow. My life was good and I was passionate about sharing yoga with others. But I still needed a guide for my practice and to help me become a teacher.

After several months of practicing on my own, I decided I wanted to make a trip to study with Matthew, an authorized teacher in Michigan. If I was going to teach Ashtanga in a traditional manner, I wanted to practice with someone who was as connected to the lineage as Laruga. There were no teachers in Ohio with that direct connection. When I was planning my trip, I happened to meet a woman from Detroit who was working in Columbus and was a longtime student of Matthew's. One day after yoga class, Lorraine overheard me talking about going to Michigan to practice. She had just moved to Columbus and hadn't sold her house in Michigan yet. Lorraine helped me get in touch with Matthew and gave me directions to his yoga shala. When I asked her to help me find a place to stay, she handed me a key and said, "Here, you can stay at my house." It felt like yet another God moment and a message telling me I was supposed to make the trip.

I thanked her profusely and finalized my plan to practice with Matthew for nine days. When I arrived at Ashtanga Yoga Michigan, the only sign that indicated I was in the right place was a little Ganesh sticker on the door. I felt a little bit like I was being admitted into something secret, and I kind of liked that. The first day I practiced there, Matthew's energy in the room made me sense his connection to Guruji. The lineage was present in that space and it was sacred. There were photos of Guruji and Sharath on the altar, and the walls were painted in the vibrant colors of India. There was a richness to the room and practicing there spoke to me on a highly emotional level. The experience was amazing.

The other thing I noticed was that the people in the shala were welcoming, even though I didn't know anyone there. All of the students were supportive of one another and were bonded through blood, sweat, and tears. Matthew introduced me to some of the students and I introduced myself to others. It didn't feel at all like a clique, which was different from some of my experiences at other yoga studios. I knew that something valuable was happening there. *We're all on the same path together.* When I imagined myself as a teacher, I aspired to foster a similar type of community.

I was very fortunate to be able to stay at Lorraine's and develop a connection with Matthew. I made three trips to Michigan and spent a total of twenty days studying with him that year. I wanted to practice with Matthew for two specific reasons. First, I wanted to get better at teaching. Second, I wanted to build a Mysore program in Columbus. I was looking for someone from his shala, either Matthew himself or one of his students, to be the lead teacher for our program. I was hoping one of them could make periodic trips to Columbus and direct us as I learned to run the program. I was looking for a mentor.

As Matthew and I chatted over coffee that first Sunday, I told him why I was there. He said, "I don't understand. You want one of my students to start a Mysore program in Columbus?"

"Yes. We need a teacher to guide us. I'll find a time and space. It's important for me to learn from someone who has studied in Mysore, India. Have any of your students been to Mysore?"

"I have multiple students who have been to Mysore."

"We have a few led classes and a decent-sized community in Columbus, but I want to build something bigger. I want to share this practice with more people, but I need some help."

Matthew gave me a puzzled look and asked, "How many other people do you think have traveled from Ohio to study with me?"

"I don't know. Five," I responded.

"No, not five. Not even one. The answer is zero. I think you're misunderstanding the situation."

"What do you mean?"

Matthew is a very direct person and what he said next felt like a punch to my stomach. "You came here to find a teacher for Columbus. You are the only one who has ever come here to practice with me. I think you are the teacher."

I was shocked by his words, but I was willing to consider the possibility that what he said was true. *Maybe he's right. Maybe this is another moment of grace when I need to let go and let be what is supposed to happen.* I was already teaching yoga and I did feel like it was my path. I just wasn't sure I was ready to run a Mysore program on my own yet. I was still working on myself and wanted a teacher who could lead the way forward.

Matthew and I continued our conversation and I told him that I began practicing yoga because I was looking for value in my life. I had material things, but I wasn't really happy. I needed to improve the way I treated others, my perspective on life, and my general disposition. I was restless, irritable, and discontent all the time, but then things changed when I started practicing yoga.

When Matthew told me that he was in recovery too, I immediately realized that God had put someone else directly in front of me to help me on my journey. *He is the exact person I need to talk to at this moment.* Matthew was both a sponsor and a yoga teacher in the same person. I used to tell the people in my recovery support group about finding yoga, the way it healed my body, opened my heart and mind, and helped me feel more like my true self. They didn't really get it though. They could see that yoga was having a positive impact on me, but they couldn't understand my experience. Matthew understood all of it.

I told Matthew, "I came to yoga because I was trying to undo my crazy."

He said, "Yoga attracts sane people and makes them happier. It also attracts crazy people and makes them sane." I knew I was definitely one of the crazy people seeking sanity.

Studying with Matthew gave me a clearer picture of exactly what an Ashtanga teacher was supposed to look like. I spent the next eight days observing his teaching and asking him questions. He was very traditional and taught in the same way that Guruji taught him during his multiple extended trips to India. Everything was on point: how he interacted with students, the words he spoke, and the physical adjustments he gave. Matthew taught me that the practice wasn't really about the poses. It was about making progress each day, on the mat and in life. I learned so much from him. As soon as I told him, "I'm sober and I'm trying to live my life right," he freely passed his knowledge along to me. Each time I visited him, my teaching improved as a result. I experienced a transmission between teacher and student that is difficult to explain. It was beyond words and actions.

Another exciting occurrence was that Matthew began teaching me the second series. I had been practicing the primary series for several years at that point. I was physically broken and put myself back together through the primary series. I needed to spend that much time with it. In Ashtanga, the primary series is meant to heal and purify the body, while the second series is designed to purify the nervous system. Starting second series felt like a huge step for me because it meant I had healed enough to move forward on my journey.

Before I left Michigan, one of the last things Matthew told me was, "You came here looking for a teacher. Taylor, I still think you are that teacher, whether you believe it or not. But if you're going to start a program based in this tradition, you need to ensure that it's authentic. You must be connected to the lineage. I can't emphasize to you enough that you need to find a way to get to India and drink from the well. You have to experience the practice in Mysore. It will give you the clarity you need to run a program. Otherwise, it won't materialize the way you hope. You can work toward authorization in the long term, but right now, you simply need to figure out how to make that first trip happen."

My response was, "Okay, I'll think about that." I didn't believe it was possible because Jess was just about to give birth to Makayla. I knew having a child was going to require a whole new level of responsibility from me. I didn't feel like I could run off to India and leave Jess alone with a baby to care for.

When Makayla was born a month later, it did change everything. I wouldn't know what to do with my life if she wasn't a part of it. She is such a bright light and always reminds me of what is really important and that I need to have humility. Jess and I had a rough time at the beginning of parenthood though. Makayla was lactose intolerant and wouldn't latch on to nurse. In addition, Jess suffered major tearing during labor. She had to take oxycodone to manage the pain for the first several weeks and really wasn't present during that period. Any time an addict has to take painkillers, it is very dangerous, just like taking morphine for my broken collarbone sent me right back to using. I had to focus on making sure Jess was alright while also taking care of Makayla, who was screaming bloody murder every night because she couldn't feed properly. I felt like I was putting out fires all over the place until Jess was herself again. It was a very difficult time, but I was continuously reminded of the miracle of Makayla's birth.

Jess and I ended up getting married a year after Makayla was born. We got a lot of pressure from our families to get married before that, but I wasn't ready to quickly jump into another marriage since I'd already had one that ended badly. I wanted to avoid making the same mistakes, and Jess understood that. She never pressured me. She said, "If you want to get married, let's do it. Otherwise, let's just take care of our daughter together." Having Makayla changed our lives for the better. Before, we did many things together as a couple, but something was missing. It felt like we were supposed to be parents. From the moment she was born, Makayla has added so much to our lives and has always been so full of energy. Being her father is a lot of work, but it is always worth it.

I remember wondering how I was going to have the money and time for a child, but I didn't realize how much space I had in my life that was occupied by stuff that wasn't serving me. Having a child helped me get my priorities in order. Once I had my own family, I was determined to do right by them. Growing up, my family was ripped apart and we still didn't spend much time together. I needed a different model for what a family is supposed to look like, and Jess's family provided that. We spend a lot of time with them and they've had a huge impact on our life. They are not perfect and they have their own issues, but they are still together. It was really nice to have that in our lives as we built our own family.

Jess and I had just gotten married at the end of my year of visits to Matthew's shala. At the conclusion of my last trip, Matthew told me that Sharath was coming to teach in New York for two weeks and I should go see him. He said, "You need to meet Sharath since you haven't been to Mysore yet. See if his energy speaks to you. Introduce yourself and tell him you want to go to Mysore." The trip to India still seemed out of reach to me, so I was excited about the opportunity to meet Sharath in the U.S. I booked my flight to New York as soon as I got home.

I'm in New York to practice with Sharath for a week. I've taken Matthew's advice and decided to get to know who Sharath is since I'm thinking about going to Mysore, India to study with him. I'm staying in a hostel so I can afford to be here. It's a piece of shit building in Chelsea with no air conditioning. I'm uncomfortable. It's only May, but it's already hot in the city.

I know I want to go to India, but I feel like I have to meet Sharath and find out what kind of teacher he is first. It's only been a couple of days, but I can already tell that the public image of Sharath is not the same as what I feel when I'm with him in person. Some people told me his teaching is rigid. But what I found when I actually met Sharath is that he is a soft, grounded, and humble human being.

We are all sitting on the floor listening to him speak during conference. Everything he says is about his grandfather, his guru. I feel so much gratitude for the opportunity to be here. I'm being immersed in the tradition. It's flowing out of Sharath and I'm blown away. I'm eating up every word that comes out of his mouth. This is not normal for me. I've always been kind of a rebel and have *never wanted to listen to suggestions or advice from anyone. But I'm humbled when I meet Sharath and willing to receive his teaching. The twelve-step program is the only other place I've ever surrendered like this. It's powerful.*

Sharath is sitting in front of a painting of Guruji as he talks. I'm grinning from ear to ear because I've found exactly what I've been looking for. He is my teacher and he will guide me into the next chapter of my life. I am going to be an active part of this tradition. I know I've made the right decision to come here and I also know that I'm supposed to go to India. I feel so much gratitude. This is my journey.

CHAPTER 22

FINDING MY TEACHER

I had a few months between booking my flight and my trip to New York. During that period, Joanie and I started teaching a daily Mysore program together. I was still working full-time, so my life became busier as my teaching schedule grew. I taught three evenings each week and Joanie taught the other three. I also began teaching a Mysore style class on the weekends at a local country club. There, I experienced another instance of grace. It was a small class, usually between two and six people. I always said the invocation to open each class. One day, an Indian student approached me after class and said, "I really like this class. It's similar to how they teach in India." I told her that I was hoping to make a trip to India soon so I could witness that for myself. Then she told me I wasn't saying the invocation correctly.

"Which words am I saying incorrectly?" I asked.

Instead of answering my question, she said, "I know a guru in Columbus named Sree Aswath. He's a Vedic scholar who teaches classes at his house. I'll connect you vie email so you can meet with him."

I was happy about the possibility of studying yoga philosophy with a local teacher, so I sent him a message right away. "I want to learn some Sanskrit and I'd like to learn the *Yoga Sutras* as well." Sree Aswath wasn't sure I was serious about learning, so he sent me to his website and told me I could find his audio recordings there. I wrote back to tell him, "Thank you, but I'm actually looking for a teacher."

He responded, "That is different than what I thought you were looking for. How about we study the *Sutras* over the summer?" As soon as he knew I wanted a teacher, he was willing to teach me. I was so grateful that I found a teacher at the exact moment I was looking to dive more deeply into a different aspect of yoga. I had read many yoga books, but I wasn't very familiar with the *Sutras*. We had only covered a few of them in teacher training. I was looking for more, and I found that in Sree Aswath. When I arrived at his house for the first class and told him that I teach Ashtanga yoga, he revealed that he is a cousin of Pattabhi Jois. *Holy crap! You mean to tell me he's right here in Columbus, Ohio?* What an amazing connection to find. *Keep going. This is another person to guide you on your path.* I became even further convinced that there are no coincidences in life.

I took classes at Sree Aswath's house every Monday evening for four years. He taught me Sanskrit chanting, the *Sutras*, the *Bhagavad Gita*, and the *Upanishads*. It was an important part of my development as a teacher. I knew I needed to understand the classic yogic texts in order to teach from a place of authenticity. And Sree Aswath was another role model for me. He is a compassionate man who is dedicated to selfless service through teaching. Sree Aswath held so much light. He taught me how to add the qualities that I felt like I lacked the most to my life.

The same is true for the next teacher who entered my life. When I went to New York to study with Sharath, I was a little star struck the first time he walked into the room. I had already heard so much about him and experienced great anticipation to meet him. When he led us in the opening chant, I felt like Guruji was there with us. I felt the depth of the Ashtanga tradition in the room and in him. I experienced an immediate sense of connection to Sharath. I knew I had found my teacher.

Sharath provided a great example of how to teach in a simple and straightforward manner, without confusing students with too many details. I learned the yoga can stand on its own. A great deal of explanation is not always necessary. I also learned that one person's pose doesn't have to look exactly like another person's pose. Each person is different and no two practices will look exactly the same. Yoga is about progress, not perfection. Sharath helped me understand that right away.

In the Ashtanga tradition, to have a teacher is to have a guide on a spiritual journey. Being taught by someone who learned directly from Pattabhi Jois was important to me. I felt reverence for Sharath because of it. Having a teacher who is that close to the light deepens the spiritual practice. The teacher represents everyone who has come before and all of the cumulative work that has been done up to that point. I believe that teachers give their energy to their students. The transmission from teacher to student is fresh and alive. It's often a nonverbal transmission that's impossible to receive when attempting to learn from books, videos, or other media.

I contemplated all of this as I walked the streets of New York and I began to realize that becoming a yoga teacher in the U.S. is far too easy. People pay a few thousand dollars and are handed a certificate to teach within a matter of months. What I'd heard about people who are authorized to teach in India is that they have to practice consistently for years. Authorized Ashtanga teachers earn the love and blessing from Sharath by putting in a large amount of hard work. It's not book or pop quiz kind of work. It's *show me your soul* kind of work. *Show me how deeply into your practice you can go. Show me how devoted you are.* It's completely different from graduating from teacher training in the U.S. You can't buy it because it's not for sale. It's only given when you work hard for it. That's the kind of teaching credentials I hoped to obtain. It's a blessing.

Practicing with Sharath in New York gave me the opportunity to understand what he was all about, which was important to me because I was being pulled so strongly in the direction of India. In his presence, I was able to do things in my practice I hadn't been able to do before. Even though there were one hundred and fifty people in the room, he gave me a few adjustments and I felt like he saw me and was paying attention to me. I found that, although I hadn't met him before, I trusted Sharath more than anyone else because his grandfather entrusted the lineage to him and because the things he said made so much sense to me. I also worked harder in his presence than I had ever worked before, and I had always worked pretty damn hard.

All of his teaching seemed so simple, yet so profound. I received an enormous amount of clarity from him.

At the end of the week, I introduced myself to Sharath and told him, "I'm going to try to make arrangements to visit you in India."

He replied, "Yes, you come any time."

"Thank you. It means a lot that you come to New York to teach us." I was grateful to have my first conversation with Sharath. I went back home feeling like I had a more meaningful understanding of both my practice and my teaching journey. I resolved to work hard at perfecting the art of teaching so that I could really earn the title of yoga teacher.

Another aspect of Sharath that really spoke to me was that he has a wife and children. Ashtanga is a system of yoga that is designed for householders, people who have families and jobs. Practitioners are not expected to become renunciates. Fitting the physical practice into one's life may require some creative scheduling, especially for parents, but it typically does not comprise more than a couple of hours each day. After Makayla was born, I was determined to maintain my daily practice, and I succeeded even through the sleep deprivation and exhaustion.

Fatherhood made my yoga practice, going to meetings, and maintaining my sobriety much more important because it became considerably more challenging to find time for all of that work. I had to double down because once I had a daughter, I wanted to be the best example possible for her. Having a child changed everything and softened me.

It would have been easy to skip many days on my mat after Makayla was born. Instead, the intensity of my practice actually increased. I also exerted more effort towards my program of recovery, self-inventory, and determining which of my behaviors were appropriate and which no longer served me. That's what we do through the twelve steps. I recommitted myself because I didn't want only to be a good person. I also wanted to be a good example to others, both as a father and as a human.

Becoming a father brought me to some important realizations. First, I never believed I could be a good dad because I thought I was too selfish. I had low expectations for myself when it came to parenting. My life was finally on track, but having a daughter was much different than the life to which I was accustomed. It required a different mindset and a different way of operating in the world. I wasn't convinced I could go there at first. It was only three months after Makayla was born when I realized that I was already doing a decent job at fatherhood. I also understood that Makayla only existed because I got sober and found yoga. She was a gift of my sobriety and my practice. Makayla was and still is one of the most important parts of my life. But, it's also important that I take care of myself enough to ensure that I can continue to be present for my children. To that end, my primary focus must be God, then the twelve steps and yoga, followed closely by family. Sometimes people are shocked to hear the order of my priorities, but it is the reality of my life. I know that I cannot have a family without the other elements. It is the only option for me.

Meeting Sharath gave me a clear example of how to balance fatherhood with being a dedicated yoga practitioner and teacher. I knew that if he could maintain that while teaching hundreds of students, I could find a way to do it in my own life. I had always kept Matthew's recommendation that I visit Mysore in the back of my mind, but I never really believed I would be able to make the trip because of my work and family responsibilities. However, once I met Sharath, I knew I had to go. *He is my teacher. I will sacrifice whatever is necessary to learn from him.* It was the first time in my life I had ever been so open and willing to have someone guide me. I credit sobriety for that because my ego was finally small enough to allow someone else to lead the way.

I was ready to say yes to the trip to India, although I wasn't certain how I could make it work. I had a wife, daughter, job, and bills to consider. I began saving as much money as I possibly could so I could afford it. I knew I needed to have tough conversations with Jess and Dad about the trip. I was a little nervous about it, but I realized that I was making assumptions about their reactions before I even asked them. I needed to stop putting words into their mouths.

When I talked to Jess, she was supportive of the idea even though Makayla would only be one and a half years old when I left. Jess knew it was going to be difficult to care for her alone. I understood that, but I said, "Jess, this is something I have to do. I have to go." She agreed and it felt like such a gift to me. I spent the next few months saving enough money so that they could be comfortable while I was away. I didn't want Jess to have to worry about paying any bills. I tried to make it as easy as possible for her.

I was relieved by Jess's response, but I still needed to get approval from work. I didn't expect that to happen because I needed to take almost two months off work. At the time, I was the general manager, working six days a week, and starting work at three o'clock in the morning each day. I was in charge of managing costs and I had made the company more profitable than ever, despite the economic downturn. It was an important job and I wasn't convinced they were going to let me go.

When I sat down to talk with Dad I said, "I want you to know that yoga is becoming continually more important in my life. I'd like you and Chuck to support me going to India to study with a teacher named Sharath. It's very important to me. I need your blessing because I can't lose my job now that I have a family."

I believed what happened next was another God moment because yoga always seemed a little weird to Dad. He was a very mainstream kind of guy, and yoga was definitely outside the norm in his mind. But he said something I never thought was possible for him to say. He looked me directly in the eyes and told me, "If you don't go, you'll regret it for the rest of your life." *Did he really just say that?* Dad had seen all that I'd been through with my addiction and then had watched me become successful at work and passionate about yoga, so of course he wanted to support me. "Do whatever you need to do in order to take care of yourself," he said. "We just want you in our lives." *The universe is conspiring to actually allow me to do this. Holy shit!* I really didn't believe it was possible prior to that moment.

I had some more work to do though because I also needed to get approval from Dad's partner. I said, "Chuck, I've been accepted to study yoga with a teacher in India. It's a great opportunity, but I need almost two months off. Yoga is changing my life and my perspective. You've seen how far I've come from where I was. I need to do this so I can continue moving forward."

Chuck said, "I agree that you need to do this. I won't stand in the way of your dream. Your job will be here when you return. I'm sure we'll be able to handle things here." He simply asked that I train someone else to fill in for me and that I be available to work from India. I was more than happy to agree to those conditions. Everything had fallen perfectly into line, so I bought my plane ticket and began making preparations for my trip. I couldn't believe it was actually going to happen.

I walk outside the airport to find a taxi. It's nine o'clock at night and my senses are immediately overloaded. There is more noise than I've ever heard. There are more taxis and more people than I've seen in my life. I've just landed in Mumbai after a fifteen-hour flight from Newark. My Indian seatmates on the plane advised me not to let anyone take my bags. But before I can resist, my bags are swept out of my hands by two little kids and placed on top of a taxi. I'm too disoriented to do anything but get inside the car.

I have a ten-hour layover before my flight to Goa, and Joanie suggested I use the time to take a taxi ride and see the city. I've already been traveling for more than twenty-four hours. My ankles are swollen and I'm exhausted and confused. I'm questioning this trip. Why did I leave my family? What is making me do this?

I don't know what to expect on the drive. I've never been this far away from home. I'm overwhelmed by the amount of dust, construction, noise, cars, and people everywhere. The streets are packed so tightly that no one is moving. I could reach out my window and grab the steering

wheel of the car next to us. I'm flipping out about my bags.
Someone is going to steal them. I realize I'm focusing
exclusively on my belongings at the moment, but there are
things in there I need.

We finally make it past the first stoplight outside the
airport and are immediately standing still again at the next
one. We're right next to the fish stall and I can smell the
putrid carcasses. The smell is so strong that I can taste it. The
fish vendor is wearing formerly white pants that are now
brown from the juice and blood of fish. His bright blue lungi
is tied up like a mini skirt and is also covered in blood. He's
chopping off fish heads on a wooden log. Oh my God. What
did I get myself into? My eyes have to be as wide as they can
possibly get.

I'm overwhelmed by the fish smell and by the
pollution. My nose and lungs are burning and I begin to
cough. It's eighty-five degrees outside and there is no air-
conditioning in the car. I feel like I'm in a hotbox. The driver
stops at the tea stall and asks me if I want some chai. It smells
amazing but I'm worried that it's not safe to drink. I lean
against the outside of the car while he drinks his tea and
smokes a cigarette. I look across the street and see a goat stall
and a chicken stall. They are as dirty as the fish stall and
smell just as terrible. There are skinned animals hanging
from ropes with their entrails cut out. I'm a vegetarian and
I don't remember ever feeling this sick to my stomach. Seeing
the meat on display grosses me out. Watching the bloody
butchers grosses me out. These things take place behind

closed doors in the U.S. Seeing them displayed in public is a whole new experience for me.

We continue back toward the airport past miles and miles of other stalls selling everything from flowers to tires. Around one corner I see a luxury hotel right next to a tarp being held up by some wooden sticks. The headlights are lighting the smog, so everything looks foggy. People are packed in shoulder to shoulder on the sidewalks. There are more people than I have ever imagined and I suddenly realize that I stand out like a sore thumb. I don't look like anyone else here. Everything is unfamiliar. It's major culture shock.

CHAPTER 23

CLARITY AND PURPOSE

I spent ten days in Goa while I waited for Sharath to open the shala in Mysore. My time there helped me become more comfortable with being in India. I practiced and relaxed a bit while getting to know a group of people who also were traveling to Mysore. They gave me lots of helpful information about my first trip. We all flew to Bangalore together and took a four-hour taxi ride to Mysore. That was as intense as my taxi ride in Mumbai. Six of us were packed into one big car with all of our luggage as we drove through Bangalore at rush hour. We were bombarded with children who ran up to the car and asked for money or tried to sell us toys. The streets were jam packed with people and cars. I saw construction everywhere and was overwhelmed by the noise.

We arrived in Mysore at night and I had no idea how to get to the apartment that Laruga helped me rent. I was traveling with a Turkish guy name Şenol, who I met in Goa. He directed the driver to my place and became my guide in Mysore. It was his second trip, so he taught me how to navigate the city and helped me settle in. He was my lifeline during the confusion of the first weeks. I can't imagine how I would have adjusted without him.

That first night, I walked into my studio apartment and collapsed onto the rock hard bed. After a few hours of restless sleep, I woke up in the morning and practiced in my room since I hadn't been able to register to practice at the shala yet. I took a bucket bath, walked outside, and realized I had no idea where anything was in the city. I spent the morning walking around to get my bearings and find places to rent a scooter and get a cell phone. I found some other yoga students at the coconut stand and learned that it was the central meeting place. They filled me in on the best and safest places to eat as well as registration hours.

Joanie had been to Mysore the previous year, so she shared all of her contacts with me, including the sober people she knew. I called a guy named Nandith who showed me around and helped me settle in. He also began taking me to meetings immediately. That was a strange experience because AA was founded in Akron, Ohio. When others heard I was from Ohio, they wanted my input on how they were doing things in India. They asked me if they were working the steps correctly. I assured them I was no expert just because of my hometown, but I was happy to help. I ended up sponsoring a couple of people during my stay in Mysore.

When I arrived to register at the shala, Sharath remembered me from our meeting six months earlier in New York. I was grinning from ear to ear when I sat down in his office and introduced myself as Matthew's student. Entering the shala for the first time felt like a dream come true. I could feel the depth and the tradition in the room. I saw photos of Guruji and his wife, Amma, on the walls. *This place is familiar. I've been here before.* The energy of the room coursed through my system and I felt as though someone was telling me, *this is exactly what you were doing in a previous lifetime. Now it's time to resume your studies.* It was an unexpected and wonderful sensation.

I was anxious for my first practice with Sharath the next morning. When I arrived a six o'clock "shala time" (fifteen minutes earlier than regular time), there were around seventy people packed into the room. I waited in the lobby as Sharath called "one more" to fill each space as it opened until it was my turn. I cautiously made my way between the other students to the spot where Sharath directed me to roll out my yoga mat. There was not the space between mats that I was accustomed to, so I had to be careful not to bump anyone during my practice. My height made that quite difficult and it took some time to adjust to the space constraints. I realized there was an entire code of tall person etiquette that shorter people didn't have to worry about. I couldn't even jump through my arms between poses the way I was used to without ending up halfway onto the person's mat in front of me. I also had to adjust to practicing in hotter temperatures and more humidity than I had experienced before. I sweated so heavily that I looked like I just stepped out of a swimming pool each day when I left the shala.

None of that bothered me though; I was just happy to be there. I quickly realized how special it was to practice in that space with other Ashtangis from around the world. During practice, it felt as though there was a vortex of power that was allowing each of us to transcend our human selves. There is a Sanskrit greeting, Namaste, which is often translated as *I bow to the divine in you,* or *the light in me sees the light in you.* For the first time, I experienced and acknowledged the meaning of the word on a really deep level. I understood the significance of folding the hands and exchanging that blessing with my teacher and with other students.

I practiced harder than I had ever practiced during those six weeks with Sharath and I reached a point in yoga where I had never been before. I was highly focused with consistent, driven energy toward a purpose. On my mat, I experienced a separation between mind and body. I felt removed from the physical experience, so it was like watching a movie as my practice played out in front of me and I connected with the other souls in the room. I was working hard and giving one hundred percent every day. That intensity made me believe I was burning away some karma as well.

I reflected on all of that as I walked back to my apartment after practice each day. *I don't even know who I am anymore.* I was releasing old behaviors and emotions and shedding tears in the process. I was doing really deep backbends with Sharath's mother, Saraswati. Backbends have a tendency to bring emotions to the surface for many people, and I was definitely experiencing that. I was pushed to my limit over and over again. *I don't know if I can go there today.* It was difficult, but I also felt very grateful, humble, and clear. There was no doubt in my mind that I was supposed to be in Mysore at that moment.

I learned so much from Sharath, even though he spoke few words. His method of teaching is so clear, simple, and efficient. There is a nonverbal transmission that happens between teacher and student in the shala. I also got to see how Sharath interacted with his family, which was very important and instructive to me. I appreciated how much he sacrificed for his students. He woke up at one thirty to practice each morning and then taught for seven or eight hours. I looked up to Sharath as a role model for selfless service and I allowed myself to absorb all that I could from him. I was simply there to learn. There were several hundred students studying with Sharath. Every week, we all packed ourselves into the shala for conference, where Sharath spoke more extensively. He gave a talk on a topic he wanted to address, then allowed students the opportunity to ask questions. It was a very special experience.

Life as a yoga student in Mysore was pretty simple. In addition to practice, there were chanting and Sanskrit classes offered at the shala. There were also opportunities to learn about philosophy, ayruveda, music, anatomy, and many other interesting subjects in the city of Mysore. And there were temples and many other spiritual sites to visit. My days were simple and consisted of eating, sleeping, practicing yoga, learning, and socializing.

I quickly made many friends in Mysore. My soul recognized that some of the other people there were on the same path as me. Although not everyone else was an addict, I understood that we had all found something deep inside ourselves that made us feel better through Ashtanga. Many of us experienced a general discontent with life that was alleviated through yoga. Our practices gave us clarity and purpose.

The entire experience was unbelievable to me. I couldn't believe I was still alive. I couldn't believe I was learning yoga. I couldn't believe I had gotten out of my own way enough to make the trip to Mysore. And I couldn't believe the series of guides and miracles I received on the journey there. When I was trying to get sober in the treatment center, I felt like my soul was just a small flicker of a flame, but in Mysore, it was burning brightly. Through yoga, I finally found a way to fill the void inside of me, and I felt like I was fully alive.

I also felt like a veil had been pulled away from my eyes so that I could view my life more clearly. It was similar to seeing color for the first time after I walked out of my second yoga class. I recognized that I was still doing things that were not serving me and that were impeding my progress. I knew I must continually work to eliminate the self-hate and other emotions that were left over from my addiction.

The entire trip to India took my breath away. *I'm walking on grace. I am in the flow.* It elevated my passion for the practice and made me even more excited about sharing it with others through teaching. I felt more connected to the tradition as I studied chanting and Sanskrit. *This is what I want to do. These things are filling my cup.* I gained a new perspective on what is truly important in life. I thought I had made some big sacrifices to travel to Mysore because I had to leave Jess, Makayla, and my job. But then I learned that some other students made sacrifices that were much greater than mine. I met people who spent their last penny in order to study with Sharath. Others traveled with as many as three children or permanently left their jobs. The practice of Ashtanga yoga is a catalyst for so much transformation that the sacrifices were worth it.

I saw a different way of living while I was in India. Being immersed in a different culture had a significant impact on me. I understood that my life was quite complicated and cluttered, and I hoped to change that. I saw people in India who appeared happy despite poverty. I wasn't very happy at the time, so seeing happiness that was outside the material realm caused a profound shift in my thinking. Previously, I was always fighting for more money and for good standing at work. In India, I resolved to find satisfaction in what I had instead of continually grasping for more. There was simplicity to my life as a yoga student in Mysore, and I wanted to integrate that into the rest of my life at home.

When I returned to the U.S., I found that my perspective had shifted and I wasn't content being there. There was a cumulative energy in the Mysore shala that made it more transformational than practicing anywhere else. I missed it. And I found it tough to reintegrate into society after being so focused on my yoga practice every single day. *How do I go back to work after that?* I wasn't interested in working in order to pay the bills because that seemed less important to me than the spiritual work I had been doing. My experiences in India had been so rich. I found Nandith, attended meetings, and worked the steps with others. I visited temples and participated in pujas. But most importantly, I spent time with myself and worked out the emotions that surfaced in my practice. It was such an amazing and spiritual unfolding that life at home seemed dull in comparison.

On the long flight home, I'm processing everything I experienced during my seven weeks in India. When I think about my past, I can hardly believe I've just spent time in the birthplace of Ashtanga yoga. How did I get here? I take myself back to the moment I first entered the shala. I want to remember every detail in order to relive it in my mind...

It's my second day in Mysore when Prakash opens the gates to the shala. I walk up the stairs, into the lobby, and tell Usha I'm here to register with Sharath. She tells me to sit down and wait with the others. I'm excited to enter the doors of the shala and to see Sharath. I sit down with the nine other people and survey the pictures of Guruji that are on the walls. I have a moment exactly like when I woke up with my head in a pot or ripped the sink apart to find a lost pill. How did I get here? How did I go from seeing people practicing in the shala on YouTube, to practicing with Sharath in New York, to committing myself to daily practice, to arriving in this place created by Pattabhi Jois and sustained by Sharath? I'm struck by how incredible this moment is.

After twenty minutes, we're called into the shala to wait in line outside Sharath's office. The windows are open and the fans are on to dry the dampness left over from morning practice. Behind the chair where Sharath usually sits on the stage hangs a picture of Shankaracharya giving his discourse on the Vedanta. To me, it symbolizes the transmission that occurs in the yoga room. I notice the clock is set fifteen minutes fast—shala time. Below the clock is a tiny picture of a young Sharath holding his daughter, Shraddha. There are large photos of Pattabhi Jois and Amma, his wife. The wall behind the altar has just been painted bright orange. The altar holds more photos of Sharath and his mother, Saraswati. A strand of blinking blue lights is draped over a large photo of Pattabhi Jois to commemorate his death nine months earlier. Everyone is still in mourning here.

I instantly feel the power of the shala. The imprint of Pattabhi Jois is here. The space hums with a vibrancy and feels like it is alive. It's more than just a room, thanks to all of the people who have passed through it. It's a living entity and is important in its own right. I feel a deep well of energy and I sense that it's Guruji. I'm so moved by the tradition that tears well up in my eyes. So much transformation is happening. I remember how different my life was just a few years ago. I can't believe I'm here.

I'm nervous and can feel my heart beating heavily when Sharath calls me into his office. He immediately recognizes me from New York. I'm amazed that he remembers my face after teaching so many students. It tells me a lot about the kind of person he is. I'm not sure how I *got here in the first place, but it is comforting to be recognized by Sharath when I didn't expect it. It provides more validation that I'm on the right path. Of course he recognizes me because he is my teacher, this is my path, and I'm supposed to be here. There could be no other way. I'm enthused and blown away by the whole experience. I am so grateful to be here...*

All of the emotions from that day return as I recall the experience. It changed me. I know there will be a second trip to Mysore. I will be back. I am inspired to work even harder at my teaching when I return home. Ashtanga should be taught this way. I'm going to do it. I want to transplant the feel of Mysore, India to Columbus.

CHAPTER 24

IN THE FLOW

I was a different person when I returned home from India. Before, everything that I'd done toward sobriety and cleaning up my life happened one step at a time. In India, I made a big leap forward. I felt so different that I could no longer identify with my old self. I was more open and honest. I was a better father. My perspective and priorities had shifted. Yoga meant more than ever to me and I felt like I truly understood the practice for the first time. Seeing Sharath's passion caused my own passion for teaching to grow. I was prepared to work hard to build a larger Ashtanga community in Columbus so that I could share the practice with more people.

Practicing with Sharath inspired me to change my teaching style to follow the tradition more closely. I wanted it to feel more authentic and I finally had an understanding of how to make that happen. I had been unclear about that before. I was teaching beginners too much of the primary series at once instead of teaching more slowly based on the individual. I was also allowing students to look at pieces of paper that told them the sequence of poses instead of teaching it to them in a way that would help them memorize it. I never saw a single sheet of paper in Sharath's classes. All instruction came directly from him. Although I wasn't yet authorized to teach by Sharath, I still felt obligated to uphold the tradition as one of his students.

From watching Sharath teach, I learned to refine my adjustments. Matthew had helped me learn how to give grounded assists and sense what the student is feeling. He also taught me how to connect with the person who was in front of me. Then Sharath helped me take all of that to a different level. His adjustments were light but effective. He gave me the help I needed, but made me do much of the work myself. Sharath was teaching me to be self-sufficient in my practice.

My teaching became less about people's abilities and more about their dedication. Commitment is important because Ashtanga is supposed to be a daily practice. *If you don't show up on your mat each day, I'm not going to give you a lot. You have to be willing to meet me half way.* In order to move forward, it's necessary to explore the possibilities and challenges every day. That is the only way growth is possible. When there are gaps in practice, it becomes difficult to gauge the progress. There is no clarity about what is happening. I came to understand that students who only practiced once a week could not see their progress and had a tendency to beat themselves up over not advancing. With daily practice, the transformation is very apparent. I learned that even when I couldn't do something, the daily attempts were the foundation for eventually finding stability and comfort in the pose. That type of growth is empowering.

That shift in my teaching took place during some pivotal years for me. I still had much work to do toward becoming healthy. I continued going to meetings, working the steps, communicating with my sponsor frequently, and trying to figure myself out. I had become much softer though. I didn't realize how well the yoga was working on me. Previously, I was unable to express any emotion except anger, and that anger was typically masking whatever was really going on inside of me. My anger was decreasing significantly, but sometimes I was still mad after my yoga practice. It brought up sorrow in me, and I walked out of class feeling anger instead. I didn't know why I was angry, but yoga was clearly bringing things to the surface that needed to be healed. I was also afraid of the significant changes I was experiencing, and I expressed that fear as anger. *I'm doing yoga and in the flow, but I'm pissed.*

Yoga was powerful and I didn't feel like I deserved it. I didn't feel worthy of being in the presence of a teacher like Sharath. I still required more cleaning up of my past and I had to clear out all of the junk that was left over inside of me. Fortunately, I was willing to listen to my teachers in a way that I had never listened to anyone. They had all put in meaningful work on themselves. I knew I also had to put in that kind of work. Sharath became my spiritual guide as I attempted to apply his teachings to my life.

The gift my yoga practice gave me was the ability to discard my limiting beliefs. *You're not good enough. You're tall and lanky when you should be more muscular. You're not handsome enough. You don't have enough money.* I told myself all of that crap many times over. Through yoga, I felt like all of the negative self-talk was being wiped away. I could start fresh. That was different from my sobriety work. I had to make a conscious effort to change externally. But the work of yoga was occurring in my soul. I was being cleansed internally and it was an intense process.

Sharath's influence was constantly with me as I started a morning Mysore program in Columbus. It began with my friend and me practicing together at five o'clock each morning. She was trying to establish a consistent practice and asked me to hold her accountable for showing up on her mat every day. I was already pretty thick into my yoga practice, so I said, "Sure. If you need that from me, I can be there every morning." We practiced together in the small yellow room where I took my first yoga class. After a few months, we decided to invite others to join us.

Soon, we had six people in the room and my friend said, "You should start teaching us. We're hearing great things about your Mysore class at the other studio."

I said, "Why not? If we can maintain six people, I'll start teaching."

For the first six months, I continued to teach evening classes at one studio and morning classes at the other. It was an incredibly difficult schedule to maintain while still spending time with my family and working full time for Dad. I moved my practice time to three o'clock so I could finish before teaching morning Mysore. It was a difficult schedule, but I made the change because it was important to maintain my own practice and because all of the teachers who I looked up to also practiced in the early morning hours before teaching. I also believed that something changed when I completed my practice each day. I was more available to my students in the room.

We named the class Morning Mysore Club and asked for a commitment from everyone. I believed that was a requirement if we wanted to build a serious community of practitioners. We asked students to sign a contract saying they would attend class a minimum of three days each week. *If you're not going to show up regularly, I'm not going to teach you.* It was similar to the kind of commitment I felt like other teachers required, even if they did not have contracts. The written contract may have been a little overboard and we soon abandoned it. But it did work in the way that I had hoped because people appreciated being held accountable.

After a few months, we had a regular group of fifteen students. I was grateful to have that many. At this studio, like at the other, sometimes the strategy for teaching new students was to hand them a piece of paper showing photos of each pose. *Why would you hand someone a piece of paper when there are only a few people in the room? Can't you tell a new person what the next pose is?* I had to make a decision not to let the paper be the teacher. I was the teacher in the room and I was determined to teach the way Sharath taught me. I also had to figure out whether I was going to use props, like blocks, straps, and blankets, to help people into poses. I decided against it because Sharath did not use props. I looked up to him so much that it felt weird to consider doing things differently from him. I eventually stopped teaching evening classes at the other studio because it was too much for me to maintain. As the morning classes grew, I wanted to focus all of my energy there. I was fully committed to building the program.

I realized that in order to do that, I had to combat all of the common misunderstandings about the practice. Many students only had experience with vinyasa classes when they showed up to their first Mysore class. Most vinyasa style classes are set to music, in contrast to the silence of the Mysore room. And instead of the one-on-one instruction and physical assists in the Mysore room, a vinyasa teacher guides the entire class through the same poses using verbal cues. It's quite common to hear a vinyasa teacher say something like, "If you don't know the pose, copy what your neighbor is doing." Mysore style teaching is very different because it is tailored to fit the individual needs of each student in the room.

It can be tough to convince a vinyasa student to try a Mysore class because Ashtanga has a reputation of being a difficult style of yoga. Of course Ashtanga is hard, but it is much more challenging to attend led classes than to practice Mysore style. It's harder when someone else is counting and taking you through the entire series right away. Giving the series to students in smaller sections in a Mysore class simplifies something that initially seems difficult. It's like painting by numbers. Painting is difficult because it requires a certain eye, a certain focus, and a certain talent. It's much easier to paint by numbers because clear direction is given. That's what we do in the Mysore room.

I decided to increase the attention I gave to beginners in the room because I saw other teachers who believed that the regular students were the ones who needed the most adjustments. That seemed backward to me. I believed it was important to ensure that more experienced students knew they didn't need an adjustment in a particular pose every day. It's okay for the teacher to stop giving adjustments in a pose when the student is able to do it independently. There was some pushback against my methods from other teachers at the studio, but I felt like I had a mandate because of what I experienced with Sharath in Mysore. Also, students were telling me things like, "I'm so much more focused in the room. My practice is really improving. There's something magical happening in Mysore class." I wasn't doing anything special or trying to reinvent the wheel. I was just there from five to eight each morning, trying to get clear with my teaching, paying attention to the needs of each individual student, and trying to make sure that my message was on point with the tradition of Ashtanga yoga.

As I became more centered and grounded in my own practice and moved closer to the tradition, I felt like my teaching improved. The positive feedback I received removed my self-doubt and gave me confidence and understanding that I was making an impact. I thought back to my first yoga classes and wanted to share the practice with as many people as possible so they could experience the transformative effects as well. I understood why Joanie hounded me so relentlessly until I agreed to try a class. It's difficult to verbalize the effects of yoga; they must be experienced. My passion for teaching carried me in the Mysore room. I felt like the words that came out of my mouth were already written; they were given to me.

Our community continued to grow. New students amazed me. *Why do they come back?* I realized that my message and the passion behind my words was what brought them back. People also returned to class because there was a feel of authenticity in the room. I was able to connect with people on a real level, and they appreciated that. There was value in the fact that all of the poses in the room are earned. *She's not more advanced than you; she's just been practicing for longer and has worked her ass off. Each one of those difficult postures was earned. You are all capable of the same thing.* It is the teacher's job to believe in students more than they believe in themselves. I could do poses that first seemed impossible, and I knew that sticking with the practice long enough would allow all of my students to experience that for themselves. But it was also important for people to recognize that life doesn't always seem fair when it comes to practicing, or anything else. "You're not able to do that pose yet. You're not there yet. Keep working." It's powerful to look students in the eyes and speak to them with such honesty.

Eventually, we dropped the minimum attendance requirement and stopped calling ourselves the Morning Mysore Club. I wanted us to be a welcoming community, not a pretentious club. All were invited to join because I believed the practice was for everyone. Previously, I felt like the message at the studio had been that Ashtanga was only for athletic people. But my message was that all people can practice. In India, I saw people of all ages and body types practicing with Sharath. It wasn't about comparing yourself to someone else. It was just about showing up on your mat and doing the best you can each day. I knew that if there was a competitive vibe in the Mysore room, it wouldn't feel inviting and many people would leave.

When I was in India, there was a community feel among the students practicing with Sharath. There was a community feel when I was practicing at Matthew's shala as well. The practitioners in Columbus were more scattered though. I wanted to bring us all together because everyone who was attracted to the practice knew it offered a way to improve their lives. We met on that common ground, similar to the common ground among members of recovery support groups. *I will make a conscious effort to create a strong and close-knit Ashtanga community. I want everyone to feel welcome and included.* I believed the passion for being a part of a community needed to be as strong as the passion behind the practice. The practice is difficult and we needed one another for support.

It was important that we got to know the people we practiced with because Ashtanga meant so much to all of us and greatly impacted our daily lives. It saved my life, after all. Everyone comes to the practice carrying some type of baggage that needs to be released. We were like-minded people. I decided it was not alright for a new student to walk into the room without being acknowledged. I made sure to greet every person. I remember going to classes in the beginning and never speaking to the people next to me. So I began organizing socials so that we could interact outside of class. When you know your friends are waiting for you in the room, it becomes much easier to get out of bed so early in the morning. I wanted us all to wake up and support one another in living the best lives possible every single day.

I continued practicing at three o'clock in the morning, which was easier certain days than others. Some days it was difficult for me because I practiced alone, and I appreciate practicing with a community too. Some days I was tired and tempted to take it easy in my practice, but that's not how growth happens. I knew that I could only continue to grow if I showed up and gave it my all every day. When I was only sleeping for an hour or two each night after Makayla was born, it would have been so easy to skip my own practice. *I have to practice too. Yoga won't transform my life if I don't.* Sometimes I tell that to other people and they roll their eyes. It's not possible to be a yogi and practice only one day each week. That's not even close to being enough.

I began telling students, "bring your ass to class," enough that it became our motto. I used the phrase because I wanted to hold people accountable, including myself. I was slow to learn that just showing up was the most important aspect of the practice. I used to think, *that was a good practice today* or *that was a bad practice today.* But I altered my thinking to, *if you just bring your ass to class, you've succeeded.* Ashtanga is about having the discipline to practice every day, whether or not you want to do it. The mind tends to invent a multitude of excuses, and sometimes it is not your friend. As a recovering alcoholic, I'm a perfect example of that. Addiction is a disease of the mind. It tells me I don't really have a disease, so I have to be reminded all the time in meetings. An Ashtanga practice is similar. It reminds me of my own struggles and ignorance. Each day that I show up on my mat is a good day.

Even though my solitary early morning practice is sometimes lonely, I've learned to use it as a time to reflect, and that is beneficial to me. It's therapeutic. Things that are therapeutic don't necessarily feel good and are not always supposed to be comfortable. It's like physical therapy. You may think it's going to make you feel better and it does, eventually. But first you have to go into the tender spots where you are injured, which can be painful. Through my practice, I become aware of the tender spots in my mind. I've learned not to listen to the stories in my head ninety-nine percent of the time. I no longer believe that my thoughts comprise my identity. That was a huge discovery for me and it may be the most important lesson I have to offer others about yoga. There is danger in identifying ourselves with our thoughts because it limits us. Our thoughts are not our reality. Our actions form our reality and for me, yoga helps me separate the bullshit stories I tell myself from what I am really supposed to do in the world. That ability is what I want my students to gain from the practice as well.

It's a few weeks into my second trip to India and things between Jess and I are really contentious. Things with Makayla are difficult too. She's acting out and doing some really dangerous things. We're struggling to know how to discipline her. Of course, the practice is intense too. It feels like the volume is turned up on my whole experience in India and on my relationship with my wife. We're spending more time together than usual and we're both shedding layers from the intense practice. We can't seem to get out of each other's way.

We've only gone to a couple of meetings, but no one speaks English, so they are not helping us. I go just to do a meditation and say, "I'm here." I know I won't learn anything and I'll probably get pissed off because I'm not getting what I need out of it. I've been calling my sponsor back home to deal with some of the anger that practice is kicking up. Jess has been emailing her sponsor. None of it is very effective. It's not wise to have a conversation with your wife about your sobriety. We can talk about it a little, but we can't get into the thick of it. It's just not good. I need my sponsor and my recovery community for those conversations. We're both really in the wrong spot with all of this.

I've hit a point of desperation tonight, so I get down on my knees and pray. I can't argue with Jessica anymore. I don't want to be angry at Makayla anymore. She's only two and a half. I feel beaten down. "God, help us figure out what we're supposed to do." I fall asleep hoping for an answer.

In the morning, I hear laughter and a raspy female voice down below. For some reason, I immediately think this woman is from California and she's in recovery. I peek over the second floor rail to see who it is. The clothes hanging on the line are in the way, so I can't see her face, but I see her arm and it's covered with tattoos. As I continue to listen, I hear ruggedness in her voice and I think she seems rough around the edges like me. Holy shit. She's in recovery. I can tell.

When I actually meet Khristine, my suspicions are confirmed. She's got long brown hair with blonde streaks, big bamboo earrings, a nose ring, is dressed in all black and is covered from head to toe in tattoos. I find out she's a punk rocker from San Francisco and is in recovery. I can hardly believe that the very next day after saying that prayer, the gift of another sober person has just been delivered to our doorstep. I'm not surprised though. She's precisely who we need at the exact moment when we need someone to break the tension. Now Jess can talk to Khristine about recovery. And we can start to have our own meetings. It's a miracle. Ask and you shall receive.

CHAPTER 25

ASK AND YOU SHALL RECEIVE

When I arrived home from India, I shared all of my stories with Jess and told her that I wanted the three of us to go as a family next time. I explained how India shifted my perspective and made me want to simplify our life together. Jess said, "I want to go. How could we do that?" Even though Jess was a little skeptical of yoga at first, she became more drawn to it as she supported me and my teaching. She saw the positive impact it had on me and how the principles of yoga symbolized the kind of life we were striving for from a recovery perspective. That was very appealing to Jess. Plus, she wanted to find an activity we could do together, so she started going to yoga classes with me. Jess wasn't a highly disciplined person, but she became more so by following me on the path of yoga. As soon as she realized that yoga made her feel better, she was sold on the practice. She developed her own commitment to Ashtanga.

I do not believe it was a coincidence that Jess established her own yoga practice. For both of us, yoga is an important part of our journey toward recovery from the disease of alcoholism. Our paths met for a reason. Jess is meant to be a part of my life. We are supposed to be a couple because we make each other better. We are supposed to have a teacher and allow that person to guide our lives so that we can be an example for others. We are supposed to spend time together in India and allow that experience to inform the rest of our lives.

As soon as Jess said she wanted to join me on my next trip to India, we began figuring out how to make it happen financially. A trip for three was going to be much more expensive. I sold my car and started driving a company car. Then we put our house on the market and ended up selling it for the asking price after only three days. We moved into my in-laws' house so we could save up for plane tickets, lodging, and everything else I would need to take Jess and Makayla to India with me. I started killing it at work when I returned to a sales position, so I received bonuses every week. *Everything is falling into place. I guess we're really supposed to go as a family.* I earned enough money for the trip and continued being paid during our three months in India. *How is all of this happening to me?* I started to understand that when I put good things in, I received good things back in return. I had some very rough years, but I suddenly had a life that was full of many possibilities.

Not everyone was as happy about my second trip to India as they were about my first. Dad's partner Chuck was the sales manager and was always pushing me to increase my sales. He viewed another trip to India—this time for three months—as a lack of commitment on my part. And that was justified because having a key player out of the country for so long was a valid thing to be upset about. I understood when he gave me a hard time about it. Before I left for India, Dad and Chuck were really unclear about whether they were going to give me my job back when I returned. I couldn't let that stop me though. I accepted the fact that I might have to find a new job after the trip.

Overall, Dad was still supportive of me returning to India. I was surprised because he really wanted me to help him advance his business. But I think Dad saw beyond that. He wanted to support my sobriety and he saw all of the positive effects that yoga had on my life.

Many of the other guys at work gave me a lot of encouragement too. When they asked me why I was going again, I told them, "I made a commitment to spend at least six months studying in Mysore. It's something I really want to do so I can become a better yoga teacher and person."

When I saw how happy they were for me, I realized that some of them viewed me as an example because I was willing to follow my passion. I heard comments like, "It's awesome that you're following your dream. I've never seen anyone live their life the way you are." I didn't think of myself as a role model though. I was simply following my path as I saw it opening in front of me.

My second trip to India was such a gift because I was able to have that experience with my family. Sharath got to know all three of us, which was important to me. He is a family man and frequently talks about the significance of family during conference. He knew that traveling to India with a family required a lot. Although I was grateful the three of us were together, Makayla was very challenging during the entire trip. She was extremely picky about what she would eat, and went on a hunger strike after we ran out of the foods we brought from home. She climbed onto rooftops by herself and ran into the houses of strangers to jump on their beds. Jess and I were at our wit's end trying to figure out the best way to parent her.

I experienced the same type of openness I felt during my first trip, but things were a bit heavier and more confusing to me. Because I was there with my family, I spent a lot of time focusing on being a dad instead of just focusing on myself. I know it sounds selfish, but to be honest, it was extremely draining to go so deeply into my yoga practice while having to parent at the same time. I didn't always feel as though I had enough energy to do both. But I was still grateful to be in Mysore and continued to feel a strong connection to Sharath. I also felt incredible stillness. In fact, the stillness and clarity may be what convinces me to return to my mat over and over again. There is simply nothing else that completely quiets my mental chatter in the same way.

Jess and I became closer to Nandith, the sober friend I met on my first trip, after he took us to a few meetings. Nandith is a sharp businessman who taught us the ins and outs of getting by in India. Sightseeing with a local was a much different experience because he offered us detailed explanations, taught us the protocol for temple visits, and translated for us. Nandith was our tour guide and drove us to see some spectacular sites. Makayla tended to fall asleep during the car rides, so that provided some respite for us. We met Nandith's family and ate pizza together. The more I got to know him, the more I saw that he is stand-up, honest guy. He ensured that no one took advantage of us and he looked after Makayla like a big brother.

Despite all of the positive aspects of the trip, Jess and I struggled. About halfway through our stay in India, we were both working on difficult postures and confronting the emotions that come along with that. I reached a breaking point when I felt terrible and didn't enjoy being in Mysore anymore. *Fuck. I just want to go home.* I felt disconnected from my sponsor and my support group. During my first trip to Mysore, I spent most of my time feeling blown away by the experience. But the second trip felt much more real, more raw, and on the verge of being too much for me to handle. I wasn't able to decompress the same way I did the year before.

I was frustrated with Makayla because of her behavior and because I didn't have the peace and quiet I had before. I was also frustrated with Jess because she was having difficulty adjusting to life in India. Jess wanted to be comfortable, but she wasn't. I made the mistake of saying things like, "Honey, you're not going to be as comfortable as you are at home. You're going to be here for twelve weeks, so take some deep breaths and chill out. You need to relax." Jess did not respond positively and was understandably upset with me. Those recommendations never sound good coming from a spouse, I realized. We had multiple fights as a result. I tried my best to help the situation, to no avail.

The yoga was working. It and the experience of being in India were bringing many emotions to the surface for both of us. We needed support, but neither of us could tolerate going to any more Indian meetings because it was so difficult to communicate. A few locals could speak English, but even that was tough for us to understand. Since it was Jess's first trip, she was really having trouble deciphering the speech she heard. I got by a little better, but it was still becoming a nightmare for me to attend the meetings. Tension was building because Jess and I were not getting along and we were struggling to deal with Makayla's dangerous behavior. Soon after Makayla ran out into the road and almost got hit by a bus, it all started to feel like more than I could handle. So I got down on my knees and asked for a break or some kind of help.

The very next day after I had that moment of prayer, I heard the gate downstairs close and then I heard a woman's voice. I looked over the edge of our patio and saw Khristine. It turned out she was staying at the same house as us, above the garage. She came into our lives at a point of desperation and became the relief valve that allowed us to make it through the remainder of the trip.

Khristine had roughly the same amount of time in sobriety as me, and we began working the steps together. We also started our own support group meetings. That was important because I needed to attend meetings for myself during that trip. I felt distant from my sponsor and I wanted to be part of a sober community. As soon as I said that prayer, I received exactly what I asked for. We ended up establishing an English-speaking meeting in Mysore which met on our patio. Both Indians, including Nandith, and other yoga students attended. Things improved for Jess and me after that. Attending meetings allowed us to release our pent-up anger and reminded us to accept others for who they were rather than who we believed they should be. Our interactions with each other and with Makayla softened because of that and because we were taking care of ourselves. Meetings affect me in a way that's similar to my yoga practice. I walk out of each with an improved perspective on life.

Once again, a community sprung up around us to support our sobriety in India. I sometimes hear that Ashtanga tends to attract addicts or a specific type of personality. I'm not sure that is true, but I do think that it attracts people who want to live differently from the norm. That is our common bond in the Ashtanga community. To find a group of people who were committed to both sobriety and yoga was a wonderful experience. I was excited to share my story at a meeting when I returned to Ohio. I felt down and out, disconnected, and was struggling to do the work of sobriety. But when I asked for help, it was given to me. It was remarkable to think that I had been part of establishing a meeting on the other side of the globe that helped yoga students and locals alike. It was further confirmation that I was on the correct path.

It's our second month in Mysore, and Jess, Makayla, and I have been visiting temple after temple. Makayla has not been easy to deal with on this trip. In moments of frustration, I sometimes think back to when we got the test result showing a high probability that she would have Down syndrome. When Jess and I got down on our knees to pray with tears streaming down our faces, we found a place of acceptance and knew that we would love her no matter what. Today, Makayla is alive and heathy, but she is also strong-willed and wild in some moments. On one hand, she's very outgoing and has an amazing personality. On the other hand, she has some really difficult streaks. She has many different faces and each one pulls me in a different direction. It's often upsetting, but I remind myself that accepting Makayla no matter what applies to everything about her.

We are all laying down in our apartment to rest from traveling on the busy roads and from the crowds and energy of the Shiva temple. Makayla seems to sense the spiritual purpose of this trip. She was definitely feeling the vibe at the temple today and has a spiritual look about her. She holds her own light. I'm looking at my phone when Makayla decides she wants some attention. She puts her forehead up against my forehead, looks into my eyes and says, "Dad, I can see your soul." I shake my head. How did I end up with such a special child in my life? Again, I flash back to our uncertainty before her birth and contrast that with everything she is today. It's a beautiful moment.

CHAPTER 26

FAMILY LIFE

Struggling to parent Makayla in India caused me to reflect much more seriously on fatherhood when I returned home. I want to be more than a disciplinarian; I want to be a good example for my children in all aspects of life. I also want to show them that there are other options besides society's view of what a normal life should look like. Many people do not follow their passions for financial reasons. I've heard artists say, "Art can't be my career because I won't make enough money." I believe that if you're really good at something, you should be able to put yourself out there and share your passion with the world. You should be exactly who you are supposed to be. You should not accept a desk job if it does not feel like your passion in life. If you do, you are wasting time. You have one shot in this life and you're going to sit in front of a computer in a cubicle? That's not what I want for my children. I want them to follow their dreams, even when that seems impossible.

I hope to communicate that lesson to them through teaching yoga and living my path. Even though I also worked in sales for years, I believe both jobs were part of my path. In sobriety, I've had to follow my passion. There is no other way. Dad was a good example of going to school, having a family, and getting a good paying job. But I want to be an example for my children of following one's passion. During my addiction, I got on my knees and prayed for a purpose in life. I needed a reason for my existence. In yoga, I finally found the answer.

That's why I continue to prioritize my own practice even when it is difficult because of my duties as a parent. Our whole family goes to bed early in order to support my schedule. It's worth it to go to bed early so that I can practice before my students arrive. My days are full, but I always make time for yoga because of what it's done for me. It's that important to me because it's changed my life. It gives me clarity when things are murky and it brings light to the darkest of days. The transformation that comes with the practice is not over for me. I continue to walk into the room and shed layers that are no longer useful to me. That's why I don't give myself any excuses not to practice every day.

It's also important for me to practice all of the ethical principles of yoga with my family. The yamas and niyamas are a design for my life and how to treat people with love and kindness. There is no better indicator of whether I'm doing a good job than how I interact with my children. Jess and I are on the same team when it comes to parenting. There is no anger, dishonesty, or violence in our household. It feels very pure. That's the only word that describes it.

And it involves not grasping for things I don't need. I want to reserve my energy for only the things that are most important in life. My focus is single-pointed these days; I've eliminated the frivolous. I'm pretty simple, so what you see is what you get. I practice, teach, travel to some workshops, and spend time with my family. I don't hang out with friends very often. That's how I avoid becoming overwhelmed by my busy schedule. I'm highly disciplined in all that I do and I find great comfort in that. It leaves no space for activities that don't serve my purpose. It's special to have that kind of simplicity, even in complex times. And it's important to me that our family eats together and makes time for one another because I remember the isolation of my addiction. Even before that, when my parents were going through their divorce, no one was around. Mom was at the bar and Dad was living with another family. I felt completely alone. I want the opposite for my children.

I've learned at least as much, if not more, about myself from simply being present for my children as I've learned from my yoga practice. Being a father requires a huge amount of patience, discipline, and willingness to do things I sometimes feel unable to do because I'm tired. But being of selfless service to my children, who can't do things for themselves, always brings me back to what is important. It grounds me. Everything I do today is about altering my schedule so I can spend more time with them, being a good example for them, and teaching them how to have the right outlook on life.

Just recently, I told Makayla, "You can start your day over at any time." She had just done something for which she needed to apologize to Jess. After she apologized and Jess accepted her apology, Makayla continued to cry about it. I said, "Makayla, you've got to stop. Your mom just forgave you. Now you have to forgive yourself."

Makayla asked, "How do I do that?"

I explained, "Go into your room, take some deep breaths, and then say, 'I forgive myself for making a mistake.' Then walk back out. You don't have to pretend like it didn't happen, but it's time to let it go and move on."

Makayla did exactly what I asked and was in a different frame of mind when she emerged from her room. It was really awesome to watch. She said, "Thanks, Dad. I didn't know I could do that."

"You can start over at any time, but you have to ask for forgiveness. Apologize to the other person, apologize to yourself for doing something wrong, and then let it go." When I was young, no one ever taught me to operate that way when I made a mistake. Now, I fess up to it, accept responsibility, and then look back into the eyes of society with a clean conscience. We allow the principles of sobriety and yoga to inform everything that takes place in our household. We're not perfect but we're working at getting better. You have to continue to work on yourself, consider your assets and liabilities, and make sure that your priorities are in check. That's the personal work that must be done. People often say that anything you put in front of your sobriety, you will lose. I believe that, and it's why I must stick with the program of recovery. I am a father today because of what I learned from the principles of the twelve steps. I'm a yoga teacher because of my sobriety. I have to maintain that in order to keep the wonderful aspects of my life today.

There are certain features of family life that help me in the morning Mysore community as well. The way I treat my own family informs the way we interact in our yoga community. It makes the whole group feel like family because it's based on the same principles, just on a larger scale. I consider the community part of my family. The students are there because they respect me as a teacher. We also care so much about one another. I want to see every person who is in the room. I have a soft spot for each student I've invested in. I believe our community is continually strengthened by my experiences as a husband and father.

It's 2:30 AM when the alarm on my phone goes off. I resist hitting snooze and plant two feet on the floor instead. I feel like God is pulling me up by the collar at this early hour. I grab my watch and phone then walk down the hall into the kitchen and turn on the espresso machine to warm up the water. I let Diyo outside and tell her to pee. I give her a large Milk-Bone when she comes back inside. I hop in the shower and spend five minutes sitting on the floor and letting the water pour all over me. I try to loosen up my body while I sit.

I dry off and then dress in my yoga clothes and a pair of sandals. I make my espresso and do some light stretching. I need to move my body a little because there's such a short period of time between resting and practicing. It's a warm summer morning, so I sit outside on the patio and look up at the stars while I drink my coffee. I spend ten minutes sitting in silence and gathering myself. I mentally organize the list of things I need to do today. This is the most important part of my early morning routine.

I get in my car and drive to the shala. I turn on the lights and the heat and roll out my mat. I briefly massage a sore spot on my back and finish my coffee. I step onto my mat and my practice starts. It's 3:30 AM.

By 5:15, the dimly lit Mysore room is half-full. We begin with a chant to clear the energy and set the right intention. The room is quiet except for the sounds of breathing and sometimes crying or laughter. The energy in here is concentrated and focused. Practically, teaching is about figuring out who needs help and when, and how to do it efficiently and in a traditional manner. But on a deeper level, it's about bearing witness. Bearing witness to transformation and so many other things. I get to see beginners start to take off in their practices and become more focused. I feel people's blocks, their struggles, and their energy, good or bad. Every day, I witness, in a very intimate way, how detrimental and how positive we can be to ourselves. Not everyone is their own worst enemy, but some of us are.

I witness progress and hard work that leads to tangible results. In here, people work their asses off and I continually see proud moments. I'm not sure I've ever been in another setting where I get to see people feeling proud without having inflated egos. They are silent victories. I witness what people are struggling with, even when it's unspoken. To see motivation, inspiration, and the overcoming of obstacles daily is incredible.

CHAPTER 27

BUILDING COMMUNITY

When Jess, Makayla, and I returned home, we didn't have a house or much of anything material. We lived with Jess's parents for a few weeks and then moved into Mom's house until our next trip to India. I felt even more disconnected from my sales job than I did after my previous trip. I was extremely sad to leave Mysore. The connections I made there caused everything about our visit speak to me on a much deeper level. I wanted to stay.

I went back to work and to teaching morning Mysore. I needed to do some rebuilding. When I left for India, we had close to twenty students each morning. It was challenging to leave a growing program, but I was grateful that I found another teacher to fill in for me. Attendance dropped a bit while I was away, so I tried to circulate our message as much as possible. Soon, some of the old students began to return, plus some new people. During the winter months, classes had between twelve and fifteen students. By April, we had twenty people in the room again.

Personally, I felt like I was a notch closer to the tradition after spending three months in Mysore. I believed I had a responsibility to teach the way Sharath taught me. I felt very different from before. *Yoga is really working.* I was no longer rough around the edges. I felt one hundred percent focused, present, and in line with the tradition. Although my communication style could still be kind of forward, "no, just do this," it was no longer aggressive. I became more persuasive. Maybe my passion for the practice was so apparent that more people came to class.

We had classes five days each week, but I wanted to add a sixth day to the schedule so that we were completely in line with the way Ashtanga is practiced in Mysore. I knew convincing the studio to do that would require current students to show up as frequently as possible. I increased my efforts to build the community, and it worked. We eventually got morning Mysore classes on the schedule Sunday through Friday. I considered each class important and gave teaching my full attention every day. We added a beginner time slot to the last hour of each class so new students would feel more comfortable walking into the room for the first time. We eventually had around forty students on Sundays and extended class from three hours to four.

The studio partners said, "Taylor, ninety percent of the people who walk into morning Mysore stick around. In other classes, twenty percent of the students stay. How are you doing it?" I didn't have an answer to their question. Maybe it was my passion or the realness of how I talked to people. Maybe it was my teaching style. One of the things that distinguished me from other teachers was that they didn't hold students accountable in the way that I did.

People were shocked by the success of our program. It was catching fire and the word of mouth that stoked the fire was powerful.

I always try my best to be a clear canvas in the Mysore room, and sustaining my own practice makes that possible. It would be easy to say, *I'm not going to practice today*. In fact, eighty percent of the time, my mind tells me I don't want to practice. But you don't get anywhere, you don't grow, and you don't learn any lessons that way. I've been taught so many things on my mat. *Why do I treat myself like such an asshole?* My whole life has felt like I've been fighting through it and now I'm learning that sometimes I need to just breathe and let go of it; I need to surrender. I'm not necessarily the kind of person who surrenders willingly. Early morning practice has been just one more thing that I've surrendered to. When I was still teaching at the old studio, I would move into a different room to finish my practice while students arrived. Each day after I finished, I looked through the window of the Mysore room to see if anyone was there. I was surprised every single time I saw a full room. Even after several years, I still wondered, *is this a dream? Is anyone in there?* It was real. W*ow, I'm really grateful that everyone shows up. Our community is strong.*

The lessons I learn on my mat inform my teaching. One of the more important messages I strive to share with my students is that we frequently stand in our own way with regard to change. At lot of times, the obstacle is not your ability, but your perceptions. We can all be our own worst enemy at times. I am no exception. When I was working on the deep second series backbend kapotasana in Mysore, I was standing in my own way because I believed the pose was impossible. When I got to it, I was still surprised I had completed the primary series. I initially didn't think that was possible either because my body was in such poor heath when I began my yoga practice. After the healing effects of the primary series, the second series was challenging me at every point.

That was especially true for kapotasana, one of the deepest backbends in the practice. It requires a great deal of flexibility in the lower back, hip flexors, and shoulders. It can be difficult to breathe in the posture, so it often brings up a lot of fear. It's also painful for many people. The energetic quality of the pose is intense and it can elicit strong emotions because it is a big heart opener. For me, it was a moment when I was forced to choose between fighting against the pose, running away from it, or surrendering to it. Kapotasana was a huge hurdle for me and I learned a lot about myself when I was confronted with it.

Kapotasana is done from a kneeling position, which appropriately sets the tone for the level of surrender that is required to get into the posture. From your knees, you bend your back and reach your arms overhead until your hands eventually touch the floor behind your feet. Then, you walk your hands towards your knees until you can grab both heels and hold the extreme backbend for five breaths. It is no joke. *This pose is not functionally possible for me. My body has all the wrong proportions. All of the damage I did to my body is resurfacing here. I will never move beyond this.* That's the story my mind told me and, for the first three weeks, I resigned myself to never being able to do the pose. I couldn't even reach my toes, much less my heels. I was sad because I believed my learning was going to come to an end since I would never be able to get into the posture. It's not an uncommon feeling.

During the fourth week, Sharath adjusted me into the pose and it literally took my breath away. I realized how much farther I had to go to reach my heels. *Holy crap. I'm that far away from it?* But it also caused me to question my assumptions about my body. *If I can get into it with his help, what's stopping me from doing it on my own? What am I missing?* I understood that there were no physical obstacles at that point, only mental obstacles. Even though it felt physical, the only real barrier to doing the pose was the story I kept telling myself. *I'm not supposed to be working on this pose yet. He's moving me along too quickly. Kapo's gonna kill me. It's too uncomfortable. Isn't yoga supposed to feel good?* No, yoga is not supposed to feel good all the time. In fact, it can feel quite the opposite. Yoga is therapeutic, and many things that are therapeutic are neither easy nor comfortable.

Sharath adjusted me into it again three days later and I began to experience a mental shift. *Maybe I can do it myself if I just pay attention to what he is doing.* I spent about two weeks thinking that I might be able to do it until I finally arrived at a place of surrender. When I discarded the old stories, I was finally able to do the pose. I went from "I can't," to "maybe I can," to "I can do this every day." The mental chatter was the enemy. Those types of lessons from our yoga can be translated into the rest of our lives. We too often block the change that is available to us by believing the false stories our minds tell us about ourselves. When we flip the switch and throw away the stories, unbelievable transformation is possible.

Kapotasana, and other difficult postures, offers a significant life lesson. The thing about kapotasana is that it's uncomfortable for many people. It's physically uncomfortable, but it can also be emotionally uncomfortable because deep backbends often bring buried emotions to the surface. I wanted to receive Sharath's blessing to teach, and I knew he would not give it to me if I wasn't willing to enter some areas of the practice that were uncomfortable for me. I eventually learned to do the pose each and every day, even in discomfort. That approach is the opposite of the way I behaved in my addiction when I used drugs and alcohol to avoid painful feelings. I couldn't face the emotions surrounding my parents' divorce, so I masked them with alcohol. I couldn't face the guilt and shame of my DUI and overdose, so I got high instead. Part of me knew I could do great things in life, but the story in my head was, *you're not good enough. You don't measure up.* I did everything I could possibly do to turn that story into reality during my addiction.

Yoga is the process of deconstructing all of the bullshit that's in our heads. It pulled me out of the belief that I wasn't good enough and wasn't a good person. The false stories are not the same for everyone. *I'm too fat. I'm not smart enough. No one could possibly love me.* They aren't all negative either. Sometimes they are grandiose. *I'm so much better than these people. Everyone is jealous of me. My ideas are the best.* Yoga helps us eliminate those thoughts and get in touch with our deeper selves. It illuminates the divine that resides within each of us. *I am this. I am not that.* We can sort that out through years of practice. Each day, I work on separating truth from fiction and the things that serve me from the things that no longer serve me. Slowly, I am moving closer to reality and a truer picture of myself. When we do this type of work over a long period of time, we are left only with the things that are truly essential in our lives. Each individual step I take grants me new insight to share with my students. That is why I teach—not to present myself as a perfect role model, but to reveal myself as a work in progress and to be real.

═══════

It's my first day assisting Sharath in the shala. My heart is pounding through my chest. I feel like the large photo of Guruji is watching me from every angle. The room is packed and it's sweaty as hell. It's 4:30 AM, so the most advanced practitioners are here, including a bunch of authorized and certified teachers. It's intimidating. There's no space to walk between the mats, so I have to time my movements just perfectly between students' poses. I'm trying to settle myself down so I don't affect other peoples' practices.

I haven't given any adjustments yet. I've got to jump in and break the ice. I'm standing in the back by the women's changing room when Dany, another assistant, and Sharath both look at me and point down at my feet. The person right in front of me is waiting for a supta vajrasana assist that I didn't see. I'm embarrassed, but I have to shake it off. I'm here to be of service. Get over it and start helping. This isn't a space of the head; it's a space of the heart. After the adjustment, I feel like I've got this. I'm completely present now. It's game on.

CHAPTER 28

BEING OF SERVICE

Each time I returned to Mysore to practice with Sharath, I gained certainty that yoga is my true path and I devoted even more of myself to the practice. I believe it is important for each of us to find our own path and follow it with dedication. Find your passion and devote yourself to it instead of wasting time on other pursuits. If money was no object, what would you be doing with your life right now? Your answer to that question is exactly what you are supposed to be doing. If there are distractions in your life that pull you away from that focus, discard them. I understand that is not a simple thing to do. It's a process that may take many years, but it's imperative that you begin today instead of waiting until tomorrow. It's about surrender and acceptance, about no longer fighting against what is meant to be.

Before I left for India the third time, my students gave me a card that astonished me. I couldn't believe some of the messages they wrote. They let me know that my teaching was having a significant impact on their lives.

Seeing those messages made me realize that I don't have a very good perspective on the impact I'm making. I'm simply working hard at following the path I'm led down each day.

Around the same time, I began to hear students say, "Taylor is my teacher." That was a strange shift for me because in the world of Ashtanga, we're often identified by who our teacher is. It felt like a big deal to me. Before, I believed I was a strong teacher, but that's as far as it went. Suddenly people were saying, "Taylor is my teacher." *Oh yeah, I guess I am.* Recognizing that shift caused another spiritual awakening for me. You need a teacher in Ashtanga just like you need a sponsor in recovery. You need a guide to show you the way. *Do as I do, not as I say.* That person needs to have the correct fundamentals that are backed up by a yoga practice. It's not necessarily about finding someone who can do all of the poses. It's really about how someone interacts with the world and lives his or her life. It's also not about perfection or finding someone to place on a pedestal. It's about finding someone who admits to being a real person with flaws. Having a guiding light, someone to point you in the right direction, is essential.

In the Ashtanga tradition, you are a reflection of your teacher too. That's why it's important to attach yourself to someone who is a good human being. Sharath is a perfect example of that. When I hear him talk at conference, I am reminded that he is about the right things—changing, living better, focusing on family. He is a role model for me and many others.

The teacher-student relationship can be an intense experience in the Mysore room. I'm able to see the true fabric of my students as well as many of their ups and downs. Dedicated students who practice with me every day allow me to see who they really are. It's impossible to struggle on your mat each day and remain hidden behind a façade. It can be scary to surrender to being known on such a deep level. You have to be willing to accept what the teacher represents and allow him or her to guide you. That can be opposite to our socialization because our society tells us we should all strive to be number one. I was certainly shaped by that belief, and I know many others who were as well. I believe that is a misguided way of thinking. Today, my perspective is different. I want to be taught by someone who is farther down the path than me. I don't need to be number one anymore.

In Ashtanga, there is a transmission that happens from teacher to student. When the teacher is directly connected to the tradition, the student is learning from the source. For me, there was a point when I didn't want what I had. I would look at someone else and say, "I want what he has." But eventually I started saying, "I want what I have." I experienced a significant progression in that area, and to be a teacher now is to be an example for others. There is a possibility that a student will look at me and say, "I want what my teacher has," or, "I want to live my life the way my teacher lives." Because I might be a role model for some, I must ensure that I'm living consistently with the principles of yoga. It was a big leap for me to become comfortable with that idea. It made me evaluate my life and all of the skeletons in my closet. I can only be a teacher now because I confronted all of them.

I'm still a work in progress though, and I continue to study with my teacher whenever I have the chance. For my third trip to India, Jess and I started practicing with Sharath as soon as he opened the shala in October. Makayla had a couple of rough patches, but overall, things were much better than the previous trip. Sharath knew our family since we had spent three months with him the year before. Jess was more comfortable and happy. We started our twelve-step meeting again as soon as we arrived and had eight people who attended. Everything about that trip was good. It felt like the way I wanted life to be, with a smooth breeze blowing through all of it.

It is always so nice to be back in Mysore and surrounded by the people there. We registered at the shala the day we arrived and Makayla immediately jumped onto Sharath's lap and made a funny face. She got Sharath to make the same face and said, "Take a picture, Dad!" It is still one of the best photos ever and it reminds me that Sharath is human too and can still laugh. The chance to see him interacting with his children and mine is such a blessing. It is important to me that my teacher is also a family man.

Makayla occasionally played with Sharath's son, Sambhav. One day, two weeks into our trip, they were playing together outside the shala before conference. Sharath allows experienced students to assist him in the shala each year. When I saw our kids playing together, I mustered up enough courage to ask him if I could assist. I said, "Sharath, I know you probably have assistants lined up for the next three months already, but if you need someone else, I'd be happy to help. I know the shala is going to be busy and it would be an honor for me to assist you."

Sharath said no because he had already told other students they could assist. I understood and was glad that I had at least put the idea out there. Two weeks later, Sharath helped me with dropbacks and when I stood up, he told me I was going to assist at four-thirty in the morning beginning the following week. I was floored. I was very honored and I felt like Sharath appreciated that I brought my family to Mysore because he knew what that required. I felt like I had a fatherhood connection with him. He knew our entire family, and that was important to me.

When I told Jess that I would be assisting, she was excited for me. We were both amazed and grateful. *This tradition has impacted my life so greatly. Now I'm going to be assisting in the shala.* Assisting was both incredible and nerve wracking, but I considered it to be further confirmation that I was on the correct path. *This is exactly what you're supposed to be doing.*

Assisting in the shala involves supporting Sharath by helping other students with poses. There are too many students in the room for one person to handle alone. It's an honor to assist, and Sharath selects people who he's training to be teachers. When you assist, Sharath really gets to know what you're made of and if you're ready to be a teacher. It's an apprenticeship. You get the opportunity to learn how to teach at what many consider to be the best yoga school in the world.

Being an assistant is very physically demanding. I assisted from four-thirty until seven-thirty each morning, took a short break, and then practiced for two hours after that. I was used to practicing before teaching, so that was a tough adjustment. It was also hotter by the time I practiced.

Sometimes it was so humid in the shala that it rained from the concrete ceiling onto my mat.

I was excited, but I also felt like I was assisting in the most high pressure time slot. Many of the most advanced practitioners were in the room at four-thirty, including quite a few experienced teachers. I remained humble and strived to do my very best. I was thankful when I received good feedback from many of the other students. It was nice to have the quality of my teaching affirmed in that way. It was also nice to feel like I was helping Sharath and being of service to the lineage. *I will assist every time if you want me to.* It was such a gift.

I didn't go into assisting assuming that I would be authorized because it doesn't always happen like that. Plus, I knew people who Sharath had asked to assist but didn't authorize. He sometimes decides that a person isn't ready for it. Before I left Columbus, I had lunch with Joanie and she said, "You're going to get authorized on this trip." I wasn't necessarily expecting it to happen though. People work hard for authorization, but it has no set criteria. Some students receive Sharath's blessing to teach after three trips and others receive it after ten trips. It's not predictable and it must be earned through blood, sweat, and tears.

After a few days of assisting, Sharath said, "I want you to come talk to me when you're done." I wasn't sure if he meant after class that day or after the month of assisting. It ended up being at the end of the month when I went to re-register. Sharath asked how many times I had been to Mysore

"This is my third trip."

Then he simply handed me a form and told me to fill it out. There were no congratulations. Balloons didn't fall from the ceiling. There was no celebration or pomp and circumstance. Instead, the message I perceived was, *this is yours because you've been working hard and helping in the shala.* I felt like Sharath expected me to know it was going to happen.

In Mysore, authorization means that you've put in the necessary work and Sharath has given you a nod saying you're on the right track. It means you've become part of the lineage. The day I walked out of Sharath's office with my authorization certificate, I was elated. *This is an opportunity for me. Sharath knows that I'm doing the right things now. I feel like he sees my soul and is happy to have me as one of his teachers.* I reflected on my time with Sharath and was grateful for his vote of confidence. I had come pretty far. I believed my teacher understood me on a very deep level. I also saw authorization as a big responsibility. I had already felt an obligation to share the tradition and uphold its standards, but I understood that the mandate was even stronger at that point.

Receiving Sharath's blessing to teach was remarkable after living wrong for so many years. Once I began living right, I was always looking for validation. I hoped for some kind of affirmation that I was on the correct path. That's exactly what authorization was for me. *My teacher has just acknowledged that I've come a long way from where I was.* It was a green light telling me to keep moving forward. Sharath had always given me exactly what I needed at any particular moment, and that experience was no different.

The day I was authorized, I told Jess I needed a bit of time by myself to reflect. I went to the Shiva temple in Nanjagud because it was a meaningful and deeply spiritual place for me. Loud music was playing and the energy was powerful. Since I was so grateful for my journey, I wanted to pay my respects to the god of yoga. I spent a couple of emotional hours there, crying at times, and just soaking in the entire experience. *I can't believe this is happening. I have received so many blessings.* Authorization symbolized all the work I had done on myself and it represented complete transformation for me.

I felt like both Sharath and the universe had my back. Things shifted in a good way. After sobriety and my family, it was the most important thing to ever happen in my life. That's how much it meant, and still means, to me. To be on a list of several hundred authorized teachers around the world answered any lingering questions I had about whether I was really supposed to be a yoga teacher. *I'm on the right path.* I knew that another door was opened and that further transformation was possible for me. My experiences with Sharath during that trip added more confidence to my teaching. I felt a renewed sense of grace when I returned home to my students. I recognized that none of it would have been possible if I hadn't first been willing to surrender to the practice, to my teacher, and to my path.

I'm writing a blog post to share my story with my students and with the Ashtanga community around the world. I never thought I would get to this point. I was ashamed of my story so I didn't believe it was a good idea to share. Plus, I'm not the spokesperson for people in recovery. Anonymity is the spiritual foundation of the entire program. Its public relations policy is not to be on the news or radio. It relies on attraction rather than promotion. I'm trying to figure out what's okay to write. I feel a lot of pressure to make sure I'm doing the correct thing. Are other people in recovery going to be pissed off? It's my anonymity I'm breaking. I'm allowed to do that as long as the right intention is behind it.

It's strange to be at this point because I never felt like I needed to share my story before. For a long time, I carried around an enormous amount of guilt. I'm over that now because I've paid my dues and made it to the other side. I'm still scared of being judged, although the more I share my story, the smaller that fear becomes. I just attended a leadership conference where we worked on listening intently to each other's stories. The woman who was my partner was in tears after fifteen minutes of listening to me speak. When

I finished, she looked me in the eyes and said, "No one has ever been that open and honest with me. Your story moved me so much. Do other people know this?" The truth is, most people outside of the recovery community do not know. Her response led me to believe that sharing my story might actually be an asset for the first time. Maybe I can help others.

CHAPTER 29

SHARING MY TRUTH

The thing I found in India, in addition to a teacher, was community. I realized I had traveled light years away from the cave of isolation in which I was living during my addiction. Community is foundational to recovery, and I understood that having a community was foundational to my yoga practice as well. I found a group of genuine, supportive, and openhearted people in Mysore. My soul immediately recognized that the people I was hanging out with were all on the same path as me. Not everyone was an addict, but through Ashtanga we had all found something really deep inside of ourselves that made us feel better. We were all trying to become better human beings. I wanted something different and I needed to dive deeper inside and work on myself to find it. In Mysore, I met a like-minded group of people who were comfortable in their own skin. That community allowed me to be as goofy, as serious, or as passionate as I needed to be. They were all being exactly who they really were and, for the first time, I felt like I could take off my mask and be exactly who I am supposed to be.

The acceptance that I felt from the community that embraced me in Mysore and from Sharath's teaching is what I wanted everyone to feel in our Ashtanga community at home. I made a deliberate effort to build a community and that continues in our shala today. We make a conscious effort to get to know one another and work hard to be a caring, supportive, and openhearted group. If you need to cry in the room, you can cry in the room. You're allowed to be whoever you really are without judgment from us. I believe that community is the most important part of our practice because we are all struggling with something. Witnessing the struggle of others and being supported in our own struggles reminds us that we are not alone. We are all working to become better people, me included. I try to provide a landscape of realness that allows everyone to be comfortable enough to shed layers and make real progress in their lives. There is something important about feeling connected to others and being seen on a really deep level that is too often missing in society. That's why our community makes yoga about the people, not the poses. I see my role as less about being the teacher and more about serving others in a caring community. Yoga has given me the opportunity to live my true purpose, which is the exact opposite of how I was living my life as an addict. Today, I'm sober and I have friendships that I never thought were possible. I'm part of a group of people who care about each other and I believe we're doing something that can have an impact, not just on our small community, but on the larger community as well. That is a beautiful thing.

I trained assistants to fill in for me during my third trip to India, and they did a spectacular job of keeping the community together while I was gone for three months. When I returned in January, I felt like the tightness of our community increased. There was a sense that what we were doing was really important and it pulled the community even closer together. I believe that what we're doing in our Mysore program is more than just a yoga class. It's a movement. I can't explain the richness that's there, but I can feel it. Everyone knows each other and there is a tightness that wasn't there when I was first learning yoga. We include everyone. We are supportive of one another. Having a strong community makes the practice that much more powerful for everyone. That kind of depth was new to our program; I didn't feel it before. The significance of what we were doing became very apparent, and the community grew.

I wanted it to grow even more to help serve more people and effect positive change in others. So I got to work figuring out how to make that happen. I promoted our program before, but I was never really comfortable with doing that and with putting myself out there. I never even took a yoga picture during the first six years of my practice. I realized that if I really wanted to achieve what I was claiming to want, I had to be willing to do whatever it took to get the word out. Getting comfortable with using social media in order to do that was a big change for me. I had to become secure enough in myself to share my yoga journey with others.

As I started putting myself out there more, our local Ashtanga community continued to grow. When I opened up to a few people about my past, they encouraged me to share my story more publically. *It's not anyone else's business. It's too dark. I can't do it. I'm too afraid.* I resisted it, but those few people encouraged me to do it anyway. Eventually, they began to convince me that I had a unique message to share with the larger yoga community because of my history. The struggle was real and gritty for me and I was encouraged by the prospect of reaching others with similar experiences.

After much thought, I took what was a giant step for me and wrote a blog about my past. I wrote and rewrote for three months because I was so anxious about it. When I was finally satisfied enough to post it, around ten thousand people viewed it and a few hundred people shared it on Facebook. Before that, I had already picked up some workshops by reaching out to my friends, but most people didn't recognize my name. My reputation as a teacher wasn't solidified enough. But after I wrote that blog, my schedule started to fill up quickly. That's not why I wrote the blog though; I actually wrote it for me. I needed to let go of the emotions around it. *If I'm supposed to do this, then I will share my story. I'm going to be open if it means I can help others.* I got out of my own way and went for it. It helped that I felt like my teacher supported me. I stopped caring what other people thought of me. *If I'm supposed to share that I'm an addict and alcoholic in recovery, then I don't care if the Ashtanga world judges me. I need to do this.*

It wasn't so difficult to give up caring what anyone else thought because I'm someone who never felt like I fit in. I wanted to create a group where no one felt like an outsider. We're all struggling with something. There is an aspect to what we're doing that is highly authentic. And I think part of that was me getting a little bit more real with the students because, when I wrote that blog, almost no one knew my story. Only three of my students were aware of my past, and two of them were my wife and sister. It was simply not something that I shared because I thought it was a liability. I had to flip that assumption though. *This needs to be shared. My story is actually an asset because everyone has their own struggles.*

I also sensed a problem in the yoga world because I believed people were often sharing superficial bullshit rather than the truth. There were a lot of beautiful photos and lofty comments that I didn't perceive as being grounded in reality. Some of it felt phony to me. I saw countless pictures with magical Rumi quotes, or sayings such as, "you are made of stardust." Social media was full of beautiful girls doing impressive yoga poses. The photos were beautiful as art, but I didn't believe they represented most people's reality. They certainly didn't represent mine. I felt like much of what I saw in the yoga community lacked realness because we weren't talking about the grittier side of life and what yoga was really doing for us. Writing that blog was about me moving closer to sharing my truth and being an example for others. Once I posted it, I received many messages from others in the Ashtanga community telling me that they identified with my experiences.

Other people started speaking their truths as well. Yes, we were showing fancy yoga poses, but the message started to be transformed. *I'm not perfect, but yoga has helped me become clearer on my path and clean up my life.* Some people wrote about eating disorders, mental illness, and suicide. Maybe it was just because my eyes were open that I was seeing more realness, but I thought it was amazing to see things move in that direction. When you become vulnerable, you don't actually know what you're going to attract. The story I told was true and I wasn't proud of much of it. There were many tears and great hardship behind it. I didn't expect the reaction I received. Suddenly, people were paying attention to our community in Columbus. I'm not sure if it was directly related to me sharing my story, but more people were attracted to our program after I put myself out there.

Our group got tight enough that the value of what we were doing became even greater for everyone. People began bringing their friends and family members. When we were approaching fifty students, I thought, *what would happen if every one of those students brought someone else who they really cared about*? It was the first time I was comfortable asking other people to invite new students. Sometimes it just happens naturally, but this was more about me being honest with a lot of the students and saying, "If this is important to you, share it with others. If you know someone who would feel at home in our group, ask him or her to come to class with you." That's how growth occurs. Our program is bigger and more important than me. *We must share this message.* I asked others to help, and many eagerly agreed.

It was a big step for me to go from being the face of the program to seeing that our community was so strong that it was supporting itself. It was also amazing to see everyone's hard work come to fruition. What began as a meager few people practicing together grew into a large and vibrant community. More people wanted to be a part of it and share what we were doing. Watching the student base grow made me understand that what we had was appealing and its potential was limitless.

Ten-month old Isaiah's tiny hand grips the front of my Ashtanga Yoga Columbus t-shirt as he sleeps in my arms. It's mid-afternoon and I'm sitting on the couch imagining the life we have in front of us, all of the things I want to tell him someday. There's been so much trauma, but also so much magic. You have parents who are living their beliefs, instead of the way society tells them they should live. Your parents are following their dreams. Our dreams are not about money. Our dreams are about living the best life possible and being an example so our children can do the same.

I'd still be teaching yoga even if I didn't need to earn a living. I would be doing the exact same thing. That's what I want for you. If you want to be an artist, you can be an artist. If you want to teach yoga, you can teach yoga. Whatever you do, you just have to be all in. It has to be about passion. You must follow your path. Don't ever waste time traveling down the wrong road or fighting against what is supposed to be. I did enough of that for both of us. Your life can be different. You can learn from my story.

CHAPTER 30

NEW BEGINNING

As our local Ashtanga community strengthened, my family became stronger as well. Jess and I grew together. At the beginning of our relationship, Jess was guarded and difficult to talk to. When I tried to get to know her, she wouldn't carry a conversation. She didn't pay attention and wasn't interested in small talk. *Does she not like me?* Jess was simply hidden behind her pain. At the time, she had no sense of self-worth. When I told her she was beautiful, it made her uncomfortable. I realized that she didn't see herself as pretty at all. Today, things have changed. Her life has blossomed just like mine has blossomed. Our relationship has added value to both of our lives. It encouraged Jess to develop a strong yoga practice and go to India. Those things were far outside her comfort zone when I first met her. I did them because I was following my path, but she did them because she believed in what I was doing. Jess was willing to allow my path to become her path and support me on it. Not everyone can do that, but it's the type of person she is. Jess was supportive of my first trip to India when Makayla was only a year old. Then she believed it would be a good idea for us to go together as a family after that. In Jess, I received the gift of the exact partner I needed in order to help me fulfill my purpose.

Jess makes a lot of sense to me and fits perfectly into my life. Our relationship is a direct reflection of our commitment to doing the right things and accepting other people for who they are. Just like my students are allowed to be who they really are, I want my wife to be whoever she is supposed to be. I will support her in anything she decides to do. We've experienced so many miracles in our life together. Having two healthy children was a miracle. Traveling to India together was another miracle. Now Jess wants to continue going to India with me. Yoga is as important to her as it is to me. It's kept both of us grounded as well as open and honest with each other. Belief in personal transformation is what runs deep in our relationship. I know I am much better with Jess than I could ever hope to be without her.

Before my third trip to Mysore, Jess started asking for another child. My response was, "No, we've had so many tough times with Makayla, I just can't imagine having another kid."

Jess was persistent though. She told me, "I can sense that our family is supposed to be bigger." She didn't understand exactly what she was feeling, but she believed that a piece of our family was missing. Jess was convinced that void was meant to be filled by another child. She could feel Isaiah's presence before he was conceived.

I eventually agreed with her and said, "If we're going to do this, it should probably be sooner rather than later." Isaiah was conceived in Bangalore, right before we flew back to the U.S. Even before we imagined him, I told Jess, "If we ever have a son, his name will be Isaiah." The name means *God is salvation.* Makayla means *resembles God.* Our children would not exist without my surrender to a higher power, my sobriety, and my decision to follow my true path.

As I continued to walk that path, our local yoga community grew enough that I felt like the natural progression was to find our own practice space. At a certain point, it was no longer serving us to practice in a mixed use studio. I believed we could create our own beautiful thing and positively affect the lives of others if we had a shala dedicated to teaching only Ashtanga. *We need our own space. I'm seeing transformation right in front of my eyes. Everyone is committed and involved and the program is growing.*

It was difficult to walk away from the studio where I began teaching and that had allowed me to build the program. I was grateful for my time there, but needed to move on. Of course, I wanted every student to remain a part of our community even though I couldn't be certain that moving to our new location would work out for each person. It was more important to me that everyone continued to practice because it was making a difference in their lives. I knew I was carrying the message and sharing Ashtanga yoga with them, but they came to class not just because of me. They came because of the transformative nature of the practice and I was just there to share it with them. I had to leave it at that, which required humility from me. *I'm not in charge. They have to choose.* Once I made the decision to open Ashtanga Yoga Columbus (AYC), I took a deep breath and let go of my concern about the outcome. I focused on making sure the students knew that their teacher loved them and was doing it for them.

Jess supported me through the entire process, just like she always does. She has become my biggest advocate. Sometime she supports my teaching more than I support myself. Jess puts a great amount of thought into everything she does. She is the exact opposite of me. When I have an incoherent thought, she turns it into a complete sentence. I have motivation and discipline, while she has organization and cleanliness. We complement each other on many different levels.

The students were supportive too, and many wanted to do whatever they could to help out with the move. Some worked to renovate the space and others donated money to fund the process. I requested help because that has been an important part of my journey. Whenever I become humble enough to ask for help, I receive what I need. That held true as we remodeled the new location of AYC. It was wonderful to witness the community joining together to build our new home.

Twenty-two students attended our first early morning class on New Year's Day. I was amazed that the room was packed despite the holiday. *I feel supported.* The renovations weren't complete yet, so things weren't perfect. The room was cold because the heating panels hadn't been installed and the fluorescent lighting was harsh. The students didn't seem to mind though. Everyone was happy to simply be together. The first practice felt light and clean. It also felt connected to the tradition. Photos of Guruji and Sharath guided us from the altar. *This place belongs to all of us.* There was an immediate shift. It was a new beginning.

Our first year exceeded my expectations. Now, our community is strong and many of the students have their own role to play in helping us continue to grow. We're working on ways to reach a more diverse group because we believe this yoga is for everyone. Our shala is about community, which is the opposite of my life in the isolated cave of addiction. That is reflected in my choice to call it a yoga shala rather than a yoga studio. Shala is a Sanskrit word for house. I want students to feel at home when they practice with us. I remember feeling like an outsider in my first yoga classes and during teacher training, and I never want anyone to feel like that at AYC. All are invited to our shala. We are a welcoming and compassionate group. *Who doesn't need that in their life?*

I know we have much more work ahead. How do we do more good in the world? How can we do more community outreach? Sobriety has given me the opportunity to live my true purpose, which is to share the practice of Ashtanga yoga with as many people as possible. At AYC, we are doing something that can have an impact, not just on our community, but on the larger community as well. It's a reflection of my own life in which I've gone from being part of the problem to a being a force for positive change.

I feel lucky that I got sober at age twenty five, but the truth is, it's never too late to do the right thing, whether you're eighteen or eighty five. It's just like when I told Makayla, "You can start your day over at any time." You can start your life over at any time too. It may require cleaning up a lot of messes. I certainly had a lot of cleaning to do. But it is possible at any time. It's not easy. It takes everything you've got. It takes getting out of your own way enough to allow change to happen. It takes finding a community of people who will support you and cutting ties with those who don't. It takes identifying your path, owning it, and dedicating yourself to following it at all costs. Nothing about transformation is easy, but it is always possible and always worth it.

My path is clearly yoga, and while I believe yoga has something to offer everyone, I know there are plenty of other fulfilling paths one can follow. For me, the principles of Ashtanga yoga and the principles of recovery are closely related. Both are truly about striving to be a better human being. I continue to put a huge amount of effort into working the steps, going to meetings, and checking in with my support group. I constantly ensure that my behavior is still in line with my recovery. Handling any situation wrong takes me one step closer to drinking again instead of one step closer to sobriety. If I'm trying to make a decision, I bounce the idea off other people and if it's not in line with my sobriety, I don't do it. There's a high level of scrutiny applied to everything I do, and it's a difficult standard to maintain. It's also hard to own my mistakes. It's much easier to avoid someone instead of admitting that I messed up. But I have to be willing to say, "I've made a mistake. My decision was wrong." Owning my flaws and mistakes is an act of humility that's required for my sobriety.

Maintaining sobriety for a long period of time is an incredibly challenging thing to do. It always requires continuous work and surrender. *Just let go*. Today, I realize that my experiences have taught me to persevere and to believe in myself. Through my yoga practice, I've learned that I can do anything I put my mind to. It's not a question of ability anymore. It's just a question of the amount of time it will take. The sky is the limit. It's an empowered way of walking through life and it's part of what makes me believe I'm an effective teacher. I understand the importance of recognizing my own potential as well as seeing and pointing out the potential in my students.

My life is about trying to improve every single day. I know how to put in the work and I know my journey is just beginning. I have a message to share with the world and I'm not scared of sharing it anymore. My story could be a liability, but I've decided to make it my biggest asset. If I had never been challenged, never had to struggle, and had never felt the depths of despair, I would not be where I am today. All of those experiences made me who I am. I wouldn't trade any of them for a different life.

Ten years into sobriety, I realize that so many miracles have occurred in my life. I've invested heavily into self-development, and it eventually paid off. When I was using, I always compared how I felt inside with how other people appeared to me from the outside. I tried to measure up to their external projections while feeling inadequate on the inside. That's not the case for me anymore. I'm comfortable in my own skin and how I appear on the outside matches how I feel inside. I am content. I did the work. It's not easy for people to go from where I was to the wonderful life I have today. People die from addiction. They die every day.

When you're first getting sober, it's difficult to envision how a different life could look. That was certainly true for me. Early on, if you had asked me if I was grateful to be sober, I would have said no. If you ask me now, I'll tell you that I realize I'm one of the blessed ones. I made it out alive. My journey has been about continuing to change, cleaning up my behavior, and being open to moving forward. Today, I'm realizing my potential and I'm still growing. I want to live the best life possible.

Every day I get on my knees and say, "Whatever your will is, allow me to do that. I'm happy to do whatever you need from me." It's a simple but profound prayer. So many miracles have happened in my life. The same thing can happen for you. My story demonstrates that, whatever your own personal trials are, you can make it to the other side and live a better life. Don't listen to your mind when it tells you that you can't change. No one is too far gone. You are worth doing all the hard work necessary. But you don't need to do it alone. Find a community that can help you, just as I did. Then work your ass off to change. Find your purpose and what you can contribute to this world, then you will find your own path away from darkness.

AFTERWORD

It's the final week of our two-month stay in Mysore. Outside on this perfect sunny day, I marvel at the city skyline against a backdrop of clear blue sky. Two tall coconut trees provide me with shade and a sense of peace. I'm spending some time alone to reflect on the blessings of this trip and the past year. Makayla is inside watching a movie while Jess is nursing Isaiah. Being here with my family again is such a gift, even though it comes with challenges. The balcony of our third floor apartment is nothing but a danger zone for a one-year-old. Isaiah constantly wants to climb the bars on the windows or the concrete stairs to the rooftop. There are no baby gates here, so we can never take our eyes off him. We had to withdraw Makayla from kindergarten in Ohio since she was going to be absent for two months. She's attending a Montessori school in Mysore and it's been difficult for her to adjust. She is homesick and misses her friends and her grandparents.

We just rang in the New Year and welcomed our nephew, Raphael, into the world. When we were in India two years ago, Amber joined us for the second month. She practiced yoga with Saraswathi, Sharath's mother. She also fell in love with Nandith, the guy who took me to my first meetings here. There are no coincidences in life. After Amber made several more trips to Mysore, she and Nandith decided to get married. In July, Amber quit her job and moved to India permanently. She is happier than I've ever seen her.

Jess has been spending a lot of time helping Amber with the baby. Raphael is Amber's second child, but she had

Tyson eighteen years ago, so she's had to brush up on infant care. And, giving birth in India was a much different experience than she had before. It seems more important than ever for us to be here right now so we can help. Mysore always feels like a second home and that is even truer this year because part of my family lives here. It's remarkable that I now have an even deeper connection to this city where I've experienced so much growth and transformation. Another miracle.

It's my fourth trip and I'm always grateful to be back to practice in the shala. I spent the first month assisting Sharath again. I learned more about how he teaches different people and gained new insight into my own teaching. It was an honor, but my body was tired from a full year of teaching. I've appreciated the past month of simply being a student and focusing on my own practice. I've also enjoyed two months of uninterrupted family time. During the past year, I spent a lot of time away from home while I traveled to teach workshops in different cities. That was difficult for all of us, especially Jess, who was frequently on her own with the kids. We have lots of family and other support in Ohio, but still, it is not easy for her. It's part of how she supports my teaching and I'm grateful for her willingness. We missed out on a lot of couple time this year. Mysore is where we are always able to reconnect and strengthen our marriage.

Of course each trip is different. What's unique about this one is that I'm not grasping for anything. Before, I was

312

seeking Sharath's blessing for our Mysore program in Columbus. Now, I'm not trying to prove anything. It's only about continuing to learn from my teacher. I know I will always be a student first. I feel more grounded with my family here. Sharath knows the importance of us being in India together and is good to us. I practice at 4:30, then Jess walks down with the kids and hands them off to me at the shala gate so she can practice. I take them home, make breakfast, and get Makayla ready for school. It's a true partnership and the practice remains vitally important to us both.

The first day of 2016 was also the one-year anniversary of AYC. I'm feeling very grateful to have such a supportive group of students and teachers who make it possible for me to do the work that I love and to spend time with my teacher in India. I had plenty of doubts when I first opened the shala, but we've had an amazing first year. I feel blessed to have the opportunity to teach some of the coolest people I know, people who I not only call students, but also friends. They are committed to helping me sustain the community and build on the larger vision of what AYC can offer to Columbus.

As part of that vision, Jess and I have decided to establish a foundation dedicated to sharing Ashtanga yoga with people who are struggling with addiction and with individuals in other underserved communities. We understand that not everyone has the resources to practice at AYC, so we want to extend the reach of our teaching to include a more diverse population. Our experiences have taught us that change is always possible and that yoga is a healing practice. We want to share a message of hope with as many people as possible. It's part of our ongoing twelfth step work.

Starting the foundation feels like the next step forward on my journey. Because I want to focus all of my energy on that and on teaching, I quit my sales job at Dad's company. That job had been so important for supporting my family, but at a certain point it interfered with my ability to be of service. Quitting was a tough decision, but I realized that Makayla and Isaiah need to witness me walk through some fear if I'm going to teach them to follow their own passions in life. Now I'm turning my back on certainty for the sake of passion. Although I am afraid, I know it will be worth it. All of my leaps forward have been. I've received a gift every single day for the last ten years of sobriety by simply being present and watching the miracles happen in my life. On one hand, I know I have traveled very far from where I was in my addiction. On the other hand, I feel like I'm just getting started. I have so much more to share with the world. I have so many things to teach my children.

Trini Foundation

A portion of the proceeds from sales of *A Way from Darkness* will be donated to the Trini Foundation, which is dedicated to sharing Ashtanga yoga with those suffering from drug and alcohol addiction and bringing the transformative practice into underserved communities. To learn more and make a contribution, please visit

WWW.TRINIFOUNDATION.ORG